WAKE UP!

How to Get Out of Your Mind,
Stop Living on Autopilot,
and Start Choosing Your Best Life

CLAUDIA VELANDIA

Published by Claudia Velandia
Calgary, Alberta, Canada
www.claudiavelandia.com

ISBN: 978-1-9992700-0-1
E-book ISBN: 978-1-9992700-1-8

Cover design by Katrina Johanson
Interior design by Dean Pickup
Edited by Arlene Prunkl
Proofreading by Caroline Kaiser
Photo of Claudia by Fela Waddy

First edition 2019

DEDICATION

To my younger self, who had the courage to look within,
work on herself, and own her life.

Get Your Free Guide and Workbook Now!

Congratulations on investing in yourself with this book.

Thank you for trusting me to be your guide on your journey.

I am delighted to offer you instant access to this free guide and workbook:

Get Out of Your Mind and Start Living Fearlessly

It will help you to begin owning and directing your life rather than allowing fear, which works through your conditioned mind and the survival mechanism of your brain, to control your actions.

Visit this link to download my free guide and get started. www.claudiavelandia.com/fearlessly

TABLE OF CONTENTS

INTRODUCTION

*"Be present, enjoy the moment,
and do the things that make you happy."*

That was the advice of my counsellor some years ago in the only meeting we had. I remember thinking, "Yeah, right. How is being fully present, in the moment, going to help me?"

I had sought support when I found myself hitting rock bottom. I was in pain emotionally. Over and over, I felt like running away from my life, leaving for another country, and starting all over again. I wasn't finding meaning in anything I was doing. I felt empty and lonely, and I didn't like the direction in which my life seemed to be heading. To distract myself from my pain, I found outlets in going out drinking and finding validation in serial dating. These behaviours were my way of self-medicating, and they became increasingly self-destructive. I was going through the motions of living, without meaning or purpose. I was mostly living in my head—thinking, thinking, and overthinking—and living my life as if on autopilot—work, home, gym, work again, party, back to work, gym, and back to partying again. I recall asking myself many times—as you may have as well—"Is this what life is all about? What am I doing here? And more importantly, what am I doing with my life?"

I knew there was more for me. I had a sense of *knowing* in my heart that my life could be more than what I was experiencing, that I could live in a completely different way. I remember thinking that *I* was the one responsible for taking the leap to get me out of the spot I found myself trapped in. I realized it was *my* responsibility to find meaning and give purpose to my life. It became clear that my happiness and well-being depended only on me. In my heart, I knew I was the one limiting myself, but I also knew I had the ability to do anything I set my mind to. I knew changes were required, and it was up to me, and only me, to make those changes. It was my life, thus my responsibility.

I decided to get out of my situation. This took me on a journey deep within myself. I read and read and watched everything possible to find a way to dig myself out of the emotional pain I was experiencing, to get out of my own way. I decided to change all those aspects of me that I didn't like and to start living a healthy lifestyle, taking care of my body, my mind, my heart, and my soul. I chose to take charge of my life, and I began looking for ways to shake off my limitations and lead a more fulfilling life.

After practising what I teach in this book, I am now living a different life, one that is easy, peaceful, enjoyable, passionate, compassionate, fulfilled, and happy. It is a way of living that is based on love and purpose, and filled with immeasurable opportunities and no limitations. It is a life in which *I* decide how far I can go in realizing my true potential. I've recognized that I have the power to direct my mind and how I choose to experience life. In the process, I've unearthed the best version of myself, which had previously been overshadowed by layers and layers of subconscious conditioning.

If you are reading this, you may be experiencing similar emotions and thoughts. Do you feel that you are limiting yourself or that something is missing in your life? Do you have the sense that there is more to life than what you are experiencing? Maybe you feel that you want to take a vacation from being yourself and run away from everything. Perhaps you have achieved all the financial success that you want and still find yourself empty. Are you one of those people who has worked all their life and forgotten about themselves along the way? Is fear stopping you from going after what you desire? Are you seeking to give meaning to your life? Perhaps you are consumed by a negative cycle of thoughts. Or maybe you are suffering from all of the above and doing anything you can to numb and distract yourself to avoid ruminating about your life.

With determination, it is possible to change just about any negative life situation and discover your limitless potential. The only things required are 1) a conscious decision to choose yourself, and 2) the willingness to do the inner work and connect with your essence. You have the power to take ownership of your life and experience it as your heart desires. You can choose to free yourself from the limitations of your mind and its conditioned influence on your well-being.

What I have come to understand from my journey within is that each of us is entirely responsible for choosing how we experience, interact with, and respond to our life and its challenges. The problem is that most of us, subconsciously, choose to live our lives from a conditioned perspective inherited from others, from our personal history, and from society. We behave based on personal experiences, societal expectations, and beliefs about ourselves that we have created in our minds. Most of us are not even aware that we harbour those concepts and act on them. We have been programmed to go through life as if on autopilot, seeking to live up to the expectations of others and seeking validation and happiness in the outside world. We are not connecting with our inner selves and true natures to give our lives direction and meaning. I have discovered that most of the time, we experience life from a place of fear, and fear can take over and direct our lives without our awareness. Fear prevents us from going after our hearts' desires, and it keeps us suffering.

Throughout my own journey, I became aware that I was suffering even more than I originally thought. I was so busy going through the motions that I didn't even realize it was happening. I was identifying myself with the behaviours of society, and my way of living mirrored those behaviours. I was hustling, often distracted, and feeling stressed, worried, and guilty. I was chasing what I was conditioned to believe was success, thinking this would make me happy and fulfilled. I thought it was normal—I saw everyone in the same boat and I didn't know any other way. Now that I am on "the other side," I can see clearly how I created my own suffering, and I can see how many others are suffering without being aware of it, thinking that this is all there is to life. They don't know any different.

I have learned, and you will too as you practise the teachings of this book, that the solution to getting out of our conditioned minds, disengaging from our autopilot behaviours, stopping our suffering, and living purposeful, happy lives is to embrace self-awareness and self-knowledge. This is done by looking within and connecting with our true essence, and by discovering our emotional triggers and mastering them. It is done by getting to know ourselves at the core and unpacking our subconscious beliefs and personal stories. It is then that we experience our true power. True power manifests itself when we are not bounced around by outer circumstances or by others' opinions and behaviours, when we are not constantly reacting to everything, when we are calm and focused at times when everyone else is buzzing. We experience our inner power when we choose how to live our life and choose how to experience it as it evolves. When we are in tune with our inner selves, we can purposefully direct our thoughts, words, and behaviours. That's the power of bringing consciousness to our lives.

Now let's discuss what you will find in this book. My intention is to take you on a journey that will help you understand what's going on in your mind so you can learn what is holding you back. My aim is to guide you to start living and experiencing a life that is beyond what your mind has yet conceived—a life without suffering and fear. I'll show you how to become the navigator of your life and develop your power to choose how to experience it. You'll learn how to use your conscious mind to create your most optimal life in a world of infinite possibilities.

We'll start by learning about the mind and the brain. My fascination with the brain has led me to do intensive personal research on the subject and to find out how its intrinsic mechanisms can subconsciously influence and limit us. Understanding how your brain works will help you recognize how it influences your mind.

You will move on to learn how you have been conditioned throughout your life and how this conditioning has been holding you back. You will also learn about your ego and how its manifestation is limiting you and causing you to suffer. You will learn how to undertake the inner work required to uncover your ego and conditioning in order to ultimately reduce or remove their influence. This inner work begins by understanding and mastering your emotions, which in turn will help you respond calmly, graciously, and appropriately in all kinds of situations, stressful and otherwise.

As you continue your journey of self-discovery, you'll learn how you can leverage the power of your mind and harness your power of choice. Finally, I'll invite you to see yourself as a holistic being so you can nourish and take care of the whole of you. You will learn how to synergistically use your whole being to achieve higher connection with yourself. You will be encouraged to live at a higher level of consciousness where you will find peace, flow, joy, love, and purpose.

Throughout the book I often use the words *subconscious* and *unconscious*. I tend to use both terms interchangeably, referring to something that lies below consciousness. The intention of my usage of *unconscious* in some parts of the book is to highlight when someone is taking an action while being unaware, as though they were sleeping. When you are asleep you are not conscious; you are unaware of what is happening around you. Similarly, most people live their lives lost in their thoughts, unaware of what is happening around them. They are acting out the motions of living, as if on autopilot. Not living in the present moment, they are allowing their lives to pass by without their conscious awareness, missing it out on the most precious moments. They are sleeping.

By now you've guessed it—the reason for the title of this book, *Wake Up!* I'm encouraging you to wake up from your sleeping, autopilot mode so you can truly start choosing your life and living it fully and with purpose.

A final thought before we jump into things. I am giving this subject matter a different spin to help you see different possibilities from a practical perspective. You may already be familiar with some of the concepts I describe, but if you are, please allow yourself to approach them with an open mind and from alternative viewpoints. New perspectives will intensify their meanings and allow you to continue your personal growth and evolution.

If you do the exercises in this book and have the courage to look within and take control of your mind, you will begin living a life removed from suffering. You will have the ability to navigate it by making conscious, positive choices, and you'll wake up to living fully, without limitations, and with purpose, joy, peace, grace, and love. You will be in the flow of life, in alignment with your essence.

You know yourself best and you are in charge of your life. You choose what to do with what you learn. I am your guide through this journey to help you live consciously, connect with your soul, achieve freedom and happiness, and truly live with intention.

Let's get started!

PART ONE

ARE YOU
IN CONTROL
OF YOUR LIFE?

CHAPTER ONE

WHO IS GIVING

DIRECTION TO YOUR LIFE?

*There is a powerful force within us, an
unilluminated part of the mind—separate
from the conscious mind that is constantly at work
molding our thought, feelings, and actions.*
—Sigmund Freud

Most people go about life with the firm belief that they are the ones giving their lives direction at any given moment. But if you think about it, how true can that be, when most of the time their minds are engaged with everything *except* their present direction? They are ruminating about the past or feeling upset about the things they don't have. They are worrying about the future, imagining scenarios, wishing to be in a different place—anywhere but where they currently are. They are focused on negative self-criticism, they want others to behave in a certain way, they are thinking of what to say next, they are seeking distraction, or they are lost in random thoughts. These people are doing everything except being in tune with the present moment and being aware of what is going on around them and within them. How can they be directing their lives when they are busy in their heads with past and future matters? It is only in the present moment that we can make choices, see possibilities, give direction to our lives, and experience them fully.

Perhaps you are one of those people—your mind is restless, jumping from thought to thought, and you are rarely calm. Your mind is so busy whirling through the motions of life, reacting (often negatively) without thinking about what comes your way that you're not fully aware of your surroundings or in tune with your deeper emotions. This reactive mode prompts you to make decisions and direct your life from a framework of mind that has become conditioned over time. You are so used to living within this framework that you don't know how to live differently, and thus you continue to perpetuate the cycle.

Your subconscious mind takes the lead in dictating the way you live when you are not engaged in the present moment. Without any effort on your part, it will direct you to respond automatically to whatever you are observing. It's similar to sleeping—you are not paying attention to what is unfolding before your senses; instead, your conditioned mind is running the show of your life on autopilot.

Let me explain, with an analogy, how your subconscious mind and your conditioning take the lead.

When you learned how to drive, you studied a driver's manual and learned the rules of the road. Maybe you enrolled in a class with an instructor, or your mom or dad taught you. You learned the mechanics of it. In the beginning, you observed everything around you, the other cars, the lights, the signs. You were fully aware of the driving process. You knew what you were doing every second on the road. You observed how your parents drove and you learned from them. They helped you practise and taught you their skills so you could eventually get your driver's licence.

So how do you drive nowadays? Are you still driving with that same extreme mindfulness, aware every second of what's going on around you? Probably not, right? You learned how to drive years ago and you've had lots of practice; it is now second nature and easy for you. You are using the skills you observed and were taught by your parents and your instructor. You drive based on what you know. You've become conditioned to driving from what you've learned and the experiences you've had while driving.

Now, think of those times when you are driving to work or somewhere else you often go. In theory, you would be paying attention to the road ahead and focusing on driving. But if you had to be perfectly honest, where is your mind as you're driving to familiar places?

For most people, the response is "I'm thinking about things." Most drivers are thinking about their lives—their problems, work, families, children, what to make for dinner, how many emails they have to answer, and so on. The list of distracting thoughts is endless. Your mind is thinking, probing, problem solving. You are having mental conversations and even arguments with yourself. But this means your attention is not entirely on the road or on driving. You are not focused on what you are doing at the moment; you are not present. You are in your mind, yet at the same time you are making critical choices and actions on the road. Your mind is very engaged but not with driving.

Later, when you arrive at your destination, you may find yourself wondering, how did I get here? You drove yourself to your destination, yet you are not aware of how it happened. But it makes sense that you don't remember. You were fully absorbed in your distracting thoughts. You've done this drive so often that you unconsciously took the same route and made the same choices along the way. You made decisions about changing lanes, taking exits, and the speed at which you were driving. You were not consciously directing your thoughts, not making decisions about the route you took, and not fully present in what was evolving in front of you.

But if your mind was busy, restless, jumping from thought to thought while you were driving, then who was paying attention to the road? If you were not conscious of getting there, who drove the car to your destination and who made all the choices along the way? Who was controlling your mind? Were *you* directing it to think about what you were doing?

The answer is that it was your subconscious mind driving the car and making most of your driving choices. You have become conditioned to driving without conscious thought. You were doing the process unconsciously because you learned how to drive many years ago and now it's second nature to you, like walking. Furthermore, you've driven that route so many times that you don't consider alternatives. You are used to it; it is now an automatic process for you.

Imagine for a moment that the car represents your life. You, the driver, represent the mind. The actions you take on the road represent your decisions, and your behaviours. In this case, who is driving the car of your life?

Just as you became conditioned in how to drive, you may be driving your life based on your conditioning. Like the driver who makes unconscious moves that steer the car, your unconscious thoughts may be directing actions that steer your life. Without your awareness, you are driving your life from your heavily conditioned mind.

Your own conditioning and your ego create the concepts you hold dear about the world—your beliefs, your values, your personal experiences, your upbringing, your memories—and the images of who you should be and what you should have. Your conditioning determines how you see yourself and creates the perspective from which you operate your life. Everything you do is performed automatically based on those concepts and the experiences you have accumulated throughout your life.

Because you spend so much time in your mind, you may not be aware that you are directing and living your life from this conditioned, unconscious perspective, largely on autopilot. Your life is a journey that is always evolving in the present, taking shape based on all the choices you make every single moment. It includes such simple decisions as choosing a thought, because being aware of a thought is itself a choice. If one pops into your mind, you can choose whether you want to engage with that thought or choose another one.

Yet you don't have to live unconsciously. You have the power to choose how to respond to the development of your life through the direction you give to your mind. In the rest of this book, you'll learn how to do that.

— KEY SUMMARY POINTS —

1 When you are not in tune with your emotions, when you are not aware of your thoughts, and when you are not consciously directing your behaviours, you are only going through the motions of living.

2 If you are not aware of what is evolving before you, most likely you are living your life on autopilot, as if you were sleeping. You may find yourself highly engaged in troubling thoughts about the past or future rather than being engaged in the present and aware of your surroundings.

3 It is only by living in the present moment that you have the power and the opportunity to give direction to your life and to be awake and aware enough to truly experience it.

4 When you allow your conditioned mind to take over your life and allow your actions to be unconsciously dictated from your conditioned perspective and on autopilot, you are limiting yourself from reaching your highest potential. Instead, you want to learn to direct your conscious mind, which in turn will direct your conscious actions.

CHAPTER TWO

THE MIND

Who is your enemy? Mind is your enemy.
Who is your friend? Mind is your friend.
Learn the ways of the mind.
Tend the mind with care.

—Buddha

The mind is an intangible part of your being. It is at play when you are thinking (consciously or unconsciously), when you are imagining, creating goals, and making decisions, and when you express your emotions or perceptions. You derive this information from what you know, and what you know is stored in your brain as memories. Your brain is the physical part of you that holds your mind's information.

Your mind plays a significant role in how you experience your life. At any given moment it is influencing your behaviours, your decisions, and your relationship with yourself and others. Your mind directly impacts your mental, emotional, and physical well-being.

If your mind is calm and peaceful, you can navigate life's circumstances and challenges with ease. If it is agitated, navigating life becomes a burden, and it's often challenging for you to find peace and happiness. You aren't able to find contentment and fulfillment even if you are surrounded by your loved ones, even if you have all the material goods you crave and all the recognition in the world. In the end, nothing and no one will bring you peace, light, joy, and love but you. This requires inner work, which starts with weeding your mind and then cultivating it while listening to your heart's guidance.

Your mind can be a source of joy and peace, or it can keep you trapped in a suffering and fearful state. If you cultivate fearful thoughts, fear is what you experience, and if you cultivate loving thoughts, love is what you experience. It follows that your mental attitude and its direction are critical factors in how you experience and navigate life.

Your mind drives your emotional state. To do this, your mind draws on the meaning you give to what you are experiencing at any given moment. You are allowing this meaning to form either consciously or subconsciously.

For example, when my ex-boyfriend unexpectedly broke up with me, I experienced a lot of pain because I deeply loved him. I was now faced with the choice of either allowing myself to wallow in the pain, or guiding my response and giving the experience a positive meaning. I chose to practise meditation, to be present, and to be grateful that I had met him. In order to learn from my experience, I chose to have an open mind. I chose to connect with my faith, which allowed me to trust that the situation held a higher purpose for me, something I would understand in the future, even though I wasn't able to see it at that moment. This positive, conscious way of dealing with the breakup led me to overcome my fear of being in a relationship; I evolved and grew in ways that I had never imagined. My other option was to fall into the autopilot mode of my mind, dwelling in the pain and focusing on the negative. I could have allowed my mind to influence my emotional state in negative ways. I could have been thinking about how much I was missing him and how I might have acted differently to save the relationship. If I had succumbed to my conditioning, I would have made myself a victim, sacrificing my power and my emotional well-being to him and to the circumstances.

This example of an impactful emotional situation illustrates that the way we experience life depends on the meaning we choose to give to circumstances that happen to us, and that we can harness the power of our minds by directing our thoughts in positive ways.

In the same way that your mind influences your emotional state during significant events in your life, it does so in your daily interactions.

For instance, when you have a conversation with a peer, a friend, or your partner, either in person or by phone or email, anything said or done that disturbs your emotions is caused by the unconscious meaning you give to the situation. A lack of awareness might cause you to react negatively to the situation. Often those reactions are autopilot responses from your subconscious mind, where you draw your meaning from. In a mind that is not directed, those daily interactions create a buildup of emotions that can severely affect your mental and physical health.

If you do not consciously guide your mind, it will continue recreating your life from your past experiences and from what you already know. It keeps you in the same cycle, having the same thoughts, emotions, and reactions, thus giving you the same results. You cannot create any change in your life if you continue recreating it from the same conditioned way of thinking.

Your mind is a powerful tool that you use to understand concepts, rationalize events, recall memories, make plans, and much more. Your mind brings information to your awareness when you request it. It visualizes, plans, and strategizes for you. Through your mind, you observe your life and analyze what you are experiencing. It allows you to identify your emotions, give them a name, and define their meaning. Your mind is exceptional, but how much of its power are you really tapping?

Through the conscious direction of your mind, you can create and transform your experiences, transcend your previous conditioning, evolve your way of thinking, and connect to the truth of who you are in order to live a wonderful life. But have you ever observed your mind and paid attention to what it is doing?

If you haven't, you are not alone. It wasn't until I started paying attention to my mind and my thoughts that I began to understand my emotions and programming and all they were doing to direct my life outside of my awareness.

Let's do a quick mindfulness exercise to help you further understand the mind in a simplified way. Follow the instructions below and see how your awareness increases. Take a timer, set it for five minutes, and read on.

1. *Sit back in a comfortable chair, plant your feet on the ground, start the timer, then close your eyes and take two full, big breaths. Then breathe normally and count your breaths to ten. Follow the air from your nose all the way to your belly while you are inhaling, and track it all the way back out while you are exhaling.*

2. *After your ten breaths, think about three moments in your life that made you very happy. Stay with them for a bit and recognize your emotions. Then think of three things in your life for which you are grateful. Stay with them for a bit and be aware of what you feel. And finally, think of three empowering thoughts that you will tell yourself as your own biggest fan and notice what emotions come up.*

3. *After you've thought those thoughts, quietly observe your mind until the time is over. Commit to finishing the full five minutes. Notice the thoughts that are coming and the patterns they form. Don't judge them or give them meaning, just observe them. I encourage you to give yourself the gift of paying attention to your mind.*

After you've finished, think about how the experience affected you. How did you feel? Did you notice that you have the power to direct your mind? When you were following your breathing, who was directing your mind? You were doing it. You were leading your mind to focus on your body in order to track your respiration in and out. In the second part of the exercise, you made the decision to think those positive thoughts. It was you who chose to bring those memories back, and you who recognized the emotions and experienced them again.

In the third part of the exercise, while you were observing your mind, you might have noticed two things: first, that observing your mind is uncomfortable because you are not used to doing it and second, that your mind perhaps showed you random thoughts that in themselves felt incessant and uncontrollable, urging you to stop the exercise, and maybe you yielded to them. Where did those random thoughts come from? Were you the one choosing them? Most likely you weren't. They showed up in your mind and in your awareness. You were not choosing those thoughts as you did earlier in the second part of the exercise.

I gave you the instructions for the exercise, but you chose to do it; it was you guiding your mind. Now you have experienced your power of choice and how you can consciously direct your mind and guide your focus. I encourage you to practise this exercise once every day, preferably in the morning, to train yourself to observe and positively direct your mind.

How often do you tap into the power you have of directing your mind? How often do you allow your subconscious to ramble through random thoughts on autopilot? If you have the authority to consciously choose what is in your mind, to be the master of your thoughts, to choose the meaning that you give to your circumstances, to choose to experience your emotions, to choose what actions to take and to choose what to focus on at any given moment, then why do you so often leave that power to your subconscious mind?

— KEY SUMMARY POINTS —

1. Your mind is a powerful tool, but you must use it consciously to leverage its power.

2. Your mind influences your emotional state. It can help you experience joy and peace, or it can keep you in suffering and fear.

3. By consciously directing your thoughts, you have the power to choose the meaning you give to your circumstances. This meaning influences your emotions, drives your actions, and can impact your well-being either negatively or positively.

4. The meaning you give to your circumstances can help you move forward from an undesirable situation.

5. You cannot change your life if you continue thinking the same way.

6. You can harness the power of your mind by guiding it in choosing your thoughts, choosing your focus, and choosing your actions.

7. Through intentional thought and reflection, you can acquire self-knowledge and self-awareness.

CHAPTER THREE

THE CONSCIOUS MIND, THE SUBCONSCIOUS MIND, AND CONSCIOUSNESS

It is only through your conscious mind that you can reach the subconscious and the Universal Mind. Your conscious mind is the porter at the door, the watchman at the gate. It is to the conscious mind that the subconscious looks for all its impressions.
—Robert Collier

Complex subjects like the conscious mind, the subconscious mind, and consciousness require a higher level of comprehension, even more so when you add the brain to the mix. I am about to explain those concepts in a simplified way, describe their intrinsic connections, and examine the influence each has in our lives. In this chapter, we will discuss these more complex aspects of the mind, and in Chapter 4 we will talk about the brain.

As human beings, we have both a subconscious and a conscious mind.

Your subconscious is the part of your mind that holds information that is not in your awareness. It contains the learned processes necessary for you to carry out such functions as driving your car without having to think of the required steps, allowing you to drive while having a conversation or singing a song. These subconscious processes are vital for navigating your life; otherwise you would be constantly thinking about every action you take, which would be very inefficient and make your life impossible to live.

Your subconscious mind is also where your personal conditioning and the manifestations of your ego are stored, and you act upon them unconsciously. When you do something unconsciously, you are acting without your conscious awareness; you are not focused on what you are doing. In other words, you are not directing your thoughts and your actions. Your subconscious mind also manifests itself when you automatically react with strong emotions in the face of a challenging situation or danger. It is also responsible for the pleasurable feelings you experience when you kiss and hug a loved one.

Your conscious mind shows you what is in your awareness. It is where you observe your thoughts, where you identify your beliefs, where you give a name to your emotions and recognize them. It is also where you understand your perspectives, where you learn new skills, where you do your reasoning, where you conceptualize new ideas, and where you plan and strategize. It is your intellect.

To return to the analogy of driving, your conscious mind is at work when you drive a new, unfamiliar route. In this situation, you cannot rely on your subconscious; you need to be cognizant of where you are so you can plan how to get to your destination. You are making decisions based on your observations.

Now think about a situation to which you reacted emotionally, only later, upon reflection, to wish you had acted differently. This experience shows you that the automatic reaction generated by your subconscious bypassed your awareness, your conscious mind.

"Oh, sorry, I wasn't thinking," you may say to excuse yourself in such situations. And yet it is true—you were literally not thinking, but acting from your subconscious conditioning.

Through your conscious mind, you can examine your past experiences and learn from them. You can discover and reframe your limiting beliefs, and you can create values and habits that contribute to your evolution, growth, and well-being. Your conscious mind can also influence your subconscious mind, enabling you to give new meaning to your past experiences and memories, or give a new definition to the assumptions you have about yourself and the world.

When you are self-aware and in tune with your inner self, your conscious mind will recognize when a reaction of your subconscious is forming, allowing you to direct it before it takes over your actions. Through your conscious mind you can choose your focus, choose your thoughts, be present, and be aware of what you are experiencing. This will allow you to give intentional direction to your actions. When you allow your conscious mind to witness your experiences, you can choose, with full awareness, how to navigate them. Your consciousness is the truth of who you are— your essence.

You have already experienced your essence during the mindfulness exercise of the last chapter (page 24). You, the consciousness within you, chose where to focus your mind. You experience your essence when you are in stillness, when you notice the comings and goings of your mind, when you observe what is unfolding before you, when you are aware of your emotional state in relation to what you are experiencing. You experience consciousness when all your senses are focused on the present moment.

Now that you understand the inner workings of your mind, let's continue in the next chapter with a discussion of how your brain works.

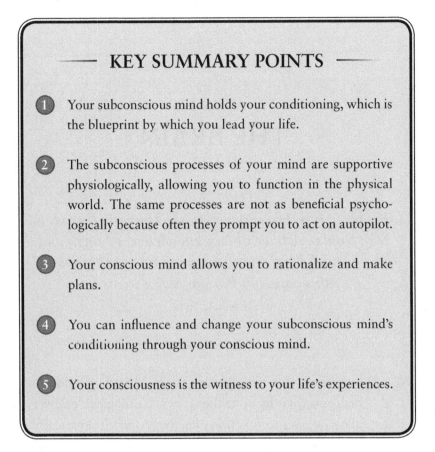

— KEY SUMMARY POINTS —

(1) Your subconscious mind holds your conditioning, which is the blueprint by which you lead your life.

(2) The subconscious processes of your mind are supportive physiologically, allowing you to function in the physical world. The same processes are not as beneficial psychologically because often they prompt you to act on autopilot.

(3) Your conscious mind allows you to rationalize and make plans.

(4) You can influence and change your subconscious mind's conditioning through your conscious mind.

(5) Your consciousness is the witness to your life's experiences.

CHAPTER FOUR

THE BRAIN

My brain is only a receiver. In the Universe there is a core from which we obtain knowledge, strength and inspiration. I have not penetrated into the secrets of this core, but I know that it exists.

—Nikola Tesla

Your brain is a complex organ composed of billions of neurons that form trillions of neurological pathways, allowing you to function effectively and automatically. It is the centre of your nervous system. It operates and coordinates most of the functions of your body and responds to any changes in your environment to ensure your survival.

Learning more about your brain and its physiological processes will help you understand more about the nature of your subconscious and conscious mind. It will help you recognize how your brain's intrinsic processes are unconsciously prompting your behaviours, guiding your thoughts, influencing the development of your conditioning—and likely causing you suffering.

The brain and the mind are connected, which means your brain can directly affect your mind and vice versa. For example, small shifts in your brain chemistry can alter your mood, concentration, and memory, which in turn will influence your thoughts, decisions, and perceptions. You can alter your brain chemistry with your thoughts.

Research suggests that we first make decisions based on our emotions, and then we rationalize those decisions. For instance, let's say you purchased something. The decision you made was based on a subconscious emotion. Once you subconsciously made that choice, your mind provided you with the rationale for it, and with your choice now justified you automatically acted to buy your item. It is essential to notice that this process provides you with a perceived sense of control. You think that you are choosing, when in reality you are deciding based on your conditioned mind.

You can alter your brain wiring through your conscious mind because the brain is "plastic," meaning it is malleable and change-able. This is known as *neuroplasticity*.

Neuroplasticity in simple terms is the ability of your brain to change its physical structure for efficiency and adaptability. Your brain is continuously being wired and rewired through your experiences, thoughts, and behaviours. Your brain has multiple neural pathways connected by neurons and synapses. Some of these pathways are used more than others, and you reinforce them further every time you feel or think in a certain way or repeat a certain action; in this way, they become increasingly entrenched. As you continue using the same pathways, they become the default paths for your brain to use, and soon the process becomes automatic, allowing your brain to work more efficiently. It is important to recognize that those deeply established neural pathways are prompting you to act or think automatically, in pre-set ways.

Since your brain is adaptable and flexible, you have the power to modify these neural pathways through conscious effort and in-tentional thought.

Furthermore, neuroscientific research suggests that your brain will do anything to protect what you have already gained. For instance, if your position at work provides you with perceived financial stability, reinforces your identity, and gives you a certain status, your brain would be threatened if you were to leave that position for the uncertainty that comes with seeking a new career. In this case, because your brain is wired to feel a sense of security, it will strive to protect your self-created identity and your perceived financial safety, preventing you from going after new opportunities. In other words, your brain is wired to be fearful of change.

The workings of your brain shape, reinforce, and influence your subconscious mind, and unconsciously this affects the way you approach life.

UNDERSTANDING YOUR BRAIN AND YOUR PROTECTION MECHANISM

Throughout your life, your senses are always engaged in bringing information from your surroundings to your brain for processing. Your brain then gives this information meaning and automatically generates a reaction to what you are experiencing. Let's use an analogy to simplify this very complex process.

Compare for a moment the brain's process to the heating system of your home. It has a temperature sensor that constantly monitors the ambient temperature. This information then goes to a processor with a program that regulates the temperature. The program compares the temperature you set to the one it receives from the sensor, and based on the outcome of that comparison, the program automatically sends a signal to adjust the temperature.

Likewise, when you observe and experience anything through your senses, the information gathered is sent to your brain, which acts as the processor and helps you interpret the world around you. It executes a program that in this case represents your conditioning. This program automatically decides what to do with the information it has received from your senses and prompts you to react accordingly.

The information gathered from your external environment with help from your senses enters your brain through the *thalamus*. This is the part of the brain that takes in all the information it receives and directs it to appropriate parts of the brain for processing.

The thalamus is the first point of entry of information. After that, your brain undertakes multiple tasks as it continues to process information in order to understand it, constructing the world that you perceive and allowing you to operate and interact with it.

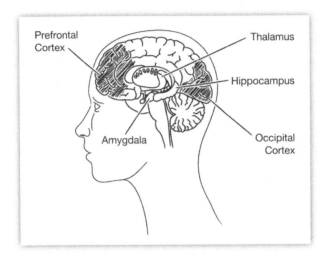

For example, when you observe something, your eyes act as your optical sensor and your brain receives the information in the form of the light waves. This information needs to be translated in order to make sense of what you are seeing. That's when the *occipital cortex* becomes involved—the part of your brain that translates the light waves and processes the visual information.

Once the occipital cortex has finalized this initial translation, it sends the outcome to other parts of the brain for further processing. The two parts that simultaneously receive this information are the *limbic system* and the *prefrontal cortex*. Let's look at the functions that these two parts of your brain perform before learning what happens when you observe something.

The limbic system is one of the parts of your brain that oversees your self-preservation. It accomplishes its function by managing your emotions, your memories, your reactions, and your bodily functions. This part of the brain originally evolved to protect you from physical harm and continued to develop to protect you from psychological harm. Two parts of the limbic system are essential for our discussion: the *hippocampus* and the *amygdala*.

The hippocampus has several functions, one of which is to encode and retrieve memories when required. Encoding means that the hippocampus creates a memory package containing everything you experienced during an event. It includes both the information you received through your senses and the associated emotions. The greater the number of links included in this package, the easier it is for your brain to retrieve a memory associated with the event you experienced. The memories that have a greater emotional impact are easy to recall because they are more prominent in your subconscious. For example, have you ever experienced a time when you smelled something, and that scent reminded you of a special moment of your life? At that moment, you quickly recalled the people involved, your feelings, and your surroundings. That was your brain at work; it retrieved a memory package with all the information associated to your memory of the scent.

The hippocampus is also ready to recall any memory of things or situations that can potentially harm you. It has a list of potential threats that it can quickly recall in order to protect you. If what you are observing is considered harmful by the hippocampus, it then triggers the amygdala.

The amygdala performs a crucial role in processing the entire range of your emotional reactions including fear, which is its specialty, and triggering your "safety system." As soon as your brain perceives a threat, the amygdala fast-tracks the fight-or-flight response. To accomplish this, the amygdala coordinates everything you need for your survival and self-preservation. It sends information to other parts of your body so you can quickly react to the threat.

The prefrontal cortex is the part of your brain that, in broad terms, executes the cognitive functions. It is where you rationalize and process your thoughts. It holds your short-term memory for quick processing while retrieving further information from your long-term memory.

Since you are overwhelmed with information every second of your life, the prefrontal cortex helps you by setting priorities, deciding what is most important for you. This part of your brain subconsciously determines what is relevant to you and ignores anything that is not indispensable for your brain or that is not in your awareness.

The prefrontal cortex also helps you with self-control. It assists you in managing and directing your impulses by using conscious thought. Through the prefrontal cortex you can override and guide the automatic flight-or-fight response generated by the amygdala.

Memories are information stored in your brain. They are not just autobiographical experiences; they also include abilities like driving your car, playing a musical instrument, doing your taxes— anything you have learned. The brain doesn't store the memories perfectly; the information stored can be altered by your own conditioning. For example, have you ever seen two people arguing about how an event took place? Both were present, yet their brains stored the information differently based on their own unique perceptions. These individual perceptions originated in each person's mind, and each of their brains stored a memory of what it considered most important.

* * *

Now that you understand the functioning of these parts of your brain and how your memories work, we can continue examining what happens when you observe something.

After the hippocampus receives the translated visual data from the occipital cortex, it compares that data with a list of threats stored in your memory. As you have learned, if what you are observing will harm you, the hippocampus will trigger the amygdala to protect you. The limbic system also receives information from other senses to obtain a full picture of what you are experiencing.

At the same time, the prefrontal cortex is processing the information that it has received from the occipital cortex, comparing it with your long-term memory. The prefrontal cortex processes the information more slowly than the limbic system, which is understandable because the limbic system is your first line of defence—it needs to work the fastest.

When all these processes are finalized, you have an understanding of what is going on around you. Your brain is subconsciously making decisions based on its interpretation of the events. This automatic process is continually scanning your physical world and assigning it meaning. The meaning is based on your memories, your programming, and the information you have at that specific time.

Let me give you an example of how this process worked to protect me. It occurred on a summer day when I was trail running in a provincial park in Canada. I was going uphill when I suddenly saw a large brown figure moving under a tree. I stopped immediately, feeling fear running through every part of my body. My heart was pounding, so I reached for my bear spray to be ready in case of a charge. Seconds later, I realized that it was a large brown cow lying under a tree, protecting itself from the sun.

This is my version of the narrative in my brain during that experience.

Occipital cortex: Guys, I see a brown figure!

Hippocampus: We're in Canada and it's summer, so it could be a bear. I've learned that bears attack people if they're surprised. Amygdala, we've got an alert—it's safety time!

Amygdala: I got this. Safety system activated and everything's ready to go. Stop! Get the bear pepper spray out and ready to use in case of a charge.

Prefrontal cortex: Hey, wait—I'm here! I've just understood what the brown figure is. It's a cow—it's harmless. We're good to go.

Amygdala: Cool! Safety system deactivated. You can proceed.

Prefrontal cortex: Awesome! Phew, that was scary. Glad it's over. Let's continue running and enjoying the beautiful day in nature.

In this example, you can appreciate how my brain quickly gave a label to the brown figure. First, based on my conditioning and my expectations, it labelled the figure as a bear and I reacted accordingly. But within seconds, my brain recognized that it was a cow and I calmed down as I realized it was not a threat.

The brain not only labels and gives meaning to potentially harmful things, but to everything you experience, and you react accordingly. For instance, let's say you recognize a certain species of tree because you have stored in your memory a clear and complete picture of that tree, and you have labelled it. Through this process, your brain provides you with the necessary information to allow you to interact with and respond to objects and experiences you encounter.

Similarly, your brain quickly provides you with a meaning for intangible experiences—things that are happening around you, such as a situation or someone's behaviour. You derive their meaning from your conditioning and from your memories. If your programming has previously labelled an experience as harmful or painful, your brain will then react to it as a threat—in this case, as a psychological threat.

PROTECTION FROM PSYCHOLOGICAL THREATS AND THE IMPACT ON YOUR WELL-BEING

Your brain has evolved to keep you safe, and it does that job very efficiently and effectively. The same mechanism your brain uses to protect you from physical threats to your self-preservation is used to protect you from the psychological ones. Your brain reacts to protect you by shielding you from emotional pain such as embarrassment, shame, sorrow, anger, frustration, and rejection, or any unpleasant emotions that will make you suffer—and you *are* suffering when you feel anything but joy, ease, grace, or peace.

Some examples of the kinds of psychological threats that manifest themselves in your brain are a career change, speaking up in a meeting, doing a public presentation, applying for a new position, receiving feedback, living in a new country, a change in relationship status, and virtually any kind of major life change.

Your brain is continually scanning for danger. Once it perceives a threat, it directs the release of stress hormones throughout your body using your automatic nervous system. It will release these hormones whether the threat is real, such as a car driving directly toward you, or perceived, such as a doing a speaking engagement in public. It's important to highlight that the perceived threat is subconsciously created from the perspective of your conditioning. For example, if you've been taught or experienced that public speaking is frightening, then that's how you will experience it going forward—unless you make a conscious effort to change that perception.

Since your brain doesn't have a built-in system that can discern whether the threat is physical or psychological, your nervous system treats them as equal—triggering the fight-or-flight response either way. The fear you experience becomes the driving force behind your defence mechanism, no matter what kind of threat you are facing. In this sense, fear has a purpose, and that is to protect your integrity. The effect of those hormones is to narrowly focus your attention on the threat. You start breathing faster, your muscles tense, and your heart starts beating quicker, preparing every part of your body to defend itself. Organs that are not essential in protecting you from the threat, such as those in your digestive system, slow down.

These stress hormones can prevent the rational part of your brain from seeing the situation as it truly is, without the benefits of your conscious awareness. In other words, the threat is bypassing your cognitive functions, and you are reacting automatically. Your rational thinking becomes clouded, impairing your ability to see more possibilities or consider different perspectives.

Psychological threats can potentially create even more fear and suffering than physical threats. For instance, imagine you have a thought such as, "I will lose my job if I don't make my sales target." Because your brain perceives missing your sales target as a threat to your financial safety, it will protect you by releasing stress hormones. In this case, your brain will protect you by doing anything it can to prevent you from losing your job. For example, it can prompt you to behave in ways that contradict your values or ethics, and it can challenge your status quo, your thoughts, and your behaviours.

Furthermore, these stress hormones can constrain your choice of options. You can become trapped by your limited perspective and react defensively toward others by imposing your opinions on them. And the release of stress hormones can impact you in other ways: your relationships with others become jeopardized, your memory becomes impaired, your immune system is compromised, and your performance and productivity are reduced.

For some people in the corporate world, project deadlines, sales quotas, and financial incentives and goals are perceived by the brain as threats. Stress hormones are released, creating motivation in the short term to increase productivity, and for some this provides a sense of accomplishment, making them feel good. The adrenalin generated by the perceived threats could become addictive and the apparent increase of productivity could become the default method of approaching business, because it could mistakenly and unknowingly be perceived as something beneficial or advantageous.

Subconsciously, you may have been operating in this survival mechanism, reacting in fear over the psychological threats that you perceive. If your body is releasing stress hormones continually, your health and well-being will be negatively affected.

TAGGING

Tagging is a term used to explain the process that the hippocampus undergoes when your brain encodes an experience or event and turns it into a memory. The emotion you feel during the experience is *tagged* by your brain in a memory along with all the information received from your senses and thoughts. By having all that information tagged in a single memory package, you are able to quickly recall all the relevant information associated with an event. And since your brain is constantly scanning your experiences, tagging allows you to react to any situation that is similar to your previous experiences faster and more efficiently. You end up making quick subconscious decisions.

Events don't have an intrinsic meaning. It is you who assigns meaning to them based on your interpretation. The interpretation comes from your own experiences and knowledge. As you give personal meaning to certain events, you tag them into a new memory package that continues forming your conditioning.

Your conditioning can be passed on to others, prompting them to similarly tag events into memory packages of their own, thus creating their own conditioning. This happens, for instance, when you share a painful experience with a friend. Similarly, you observe what others are experiencing and you tag that experience—whether painful or pleasurable—directly in your own memory package. As part of this process, your brain learns what is painful or pleasurable and teaches you what to avoid and what to seek out.

Tagging can be demonstrated using the example of a pot boiling on the stovetop. As a child, before you touched a hot pot, it was not tagged in your brain as a harmful thing. It was only when you touched it and burned yourself that you tagged it as hurtful as you experienced it. From then on, your mind automatically directed you to act with caution so you wouldn't do it again. You didn't repeat the painful experience because you had internalized the concept the first time. You now have an automatic reaction every time you perceive a hot pot, and you don't have to make a conscious decision to avoid the pain.

Similarly, this automatic reaction manifests itself when your brain perceives anything that is scalding hot. You don't have to get burned again because you have learned through association that hot equals pain regardless of the source.

The process of tagging also happens with psychological experiences. For instance, one psychological threat that your brain protects you from is the potential for rejection. You might have learned this when you were young. It could have occurred because you were rejected by someone you liked or watched others being painfully rejected. Your brain has internalized the meaning of rejection by tagging it with pain. In order to avoid similar painful situations, your brain will unconsciously and therefore automatically direct your behaviours when it perceives the possibility of rejection. Such experiences might occur when you are faced with attending a networking event, making a cold call, applying for a new job, or asking someone on a first date.

CONTROL

Your brain craves control because it allows you to stay safe and maintain your physical and psychological well-being. For instance, your brain sends signals to your body to begin shivering when you are cold so you can warm up. The sensation you feel prompts you to put on some warm clothing. In the same way that your brain triggers your body for physical protection, it triggers your mind.

If a situation in your life is out of your control—perhaps it is changing something habitual, threatening your finances, or jeopardizing the way you perceive yourself—your brain will strive to control the situation by causing you to feel unpleasant emotions. The purpose of those emotions is to drive you to maintain the status quo so your perceived equilibrium remains intact. To keep your inner world in balance, you may find yourself seeking to control circumstances and other people's behaviours.

As a human being, you have the ability to imagine the future and to create expectations and goals for yourself. These goals and expectations give direction and guidance to your life, and your mind will stubbornly cling to them. However, if your life unfolds in a way that is not in accordance with your mental picture, you will seek to manipulate the situation to obtain your desired outcome.

Subconsciously, your ego and your conditioning have you seeking to control external circumstances as well as present and future expectations. When you find you can't control these things, you suffer from psychological and physical stress. Without your conscious awareness, you are bounced around by your emotional reactions as your ego attempts to stick to these conditioned expectations. All these perceived attachments that you have no control over can cause you unnecessary suffering and keep you blind to any other possibilities that might arise.

As you seek control, you are in your brain's survival mechanism, and paradoxically, in that moment, you are out of control. This may happen when you panic, and it can lead to misinterpreting situations, missing opportunities, forming assumptions, and making poor decisions.

You no doubt know that you can't control others, and often you can't control your circumstances. You only have control over you, your mind, and what is going on within yourself.

PATTERNS

Your brain learns through patterns and also makes decisions based on them. It creates those patterns for increased efficiency. But how does this work?

It begins with your brain taking in information from your environment through your senses. This information activates and matches specific content in your long-term memory, which helps you interact with your current experience and predict what is coming next. The process of pattern creation allows you to perform actions and activities without you having to think about what your next steps will be. It helps you predict behaviours and learn new skills, and it influences the creation of your habits.

When you form a habit, your brain gradually creates an associated neural pathway that becomes deeper every time you engage in the habit. Over time, the pathway becomes so entrenched that the habit is easily, readily accessible for you. Your brain enjoys and craves the rewards it obtains from the habit, and therefore urges you to satisfy the craving. Eventually, a learned pattern emerges that is executed automatically.

Regular activities such as eating at a specific time, having your coffee, brushing your teeth, choosing particular foods, and so on are not the only habits you perform. Habits also manifest themselves in your mind, for instance, when you are leading a meeting, when you are responding to an email, or when you are choosing your words.

You may have behavioural and psychological habits that are not supporting you. We all know examples of poor habits—smoking, overeating, interrupting, procrastinating, being late, criticizing, and just about anything that affects your life negatively. You probably created any negative habits subconsciously, and unless you consciously rein them in, they will continue to control you.

NEGATIVE BIAS

Your brain has a natural tendency to want to protect you. This defence mechanism works by focusing on the negative aspect of any situation or encounter and highlighting any threats it perceives.

Since your brain innately works to keep you safe, your inclination is to look toward the future, focusing on what might cause you harm so that you can be prepared for it and avoid it if possible. Subconsciously, your brain is prompting you to feel apprehensive or afraid of situations in an imaginary future, focusing only on what could go wrong. This fearful response then becomes your default mechanism when dealing with any circumstances, causing you to approach life with an overall negative outlook.

In this protection pattern, you quickly recall memories of other negative experiences; as a result, you reinforce these memories and strengthen their negative neural pathways. For instance, imagine you've had some negative experiences while interacting with a certain company. Even though your last interaction was positive and success-ful, you will likely be focused on the negative in your next interaction. Your negative bias will influence how you perceive the company's ability to perform and how you manage your relationship with them.

This inherent bias can cause you to live in fearful states and view the world around you as full of psychological threats. If you are not self-aware, you will continue harbouring a subconscious negative bias, making you feel anxious, worried about the future and ruminating about the past. This bias prevents you from living in the present moment because your mind is busy with unproductive thoughts.

When you notice that your mind is gravitating toward its nat-ural negative bias, you can redirect it through conscious thought. If the threat is in the future, you have the power to bypass the negative bias, assess how real the threat is, and focus instead on positive possibilities. If you are ruminating about a past event, you can learn from your experience; you cannot change the past, but you can grow from it.

FILLING THE GAPS

Your senses don't provide your brain with a full picture of what you are experiencing. Your brain fills those gaps with your memories, expectations, or autobiographical experiences.

Let's take your ability to see. When you observe an object from only one angle, your brain is able to fill the gaps, which is beneficial to your comprehension. It allows you to recognize an object or a situation despite having incomplete visual information. Your brain fills the gaps by replacing the missing information with some content from your previously acquired memory. For instance, you can identify a chair, even one you have never seen, when you look at it from just a single viewpoint because you have already learned what a chair looks like.

Likewise, your brain accomplishes its gap-filling with ideas or concepts that you have already internalized. For example, imagine you're at a business networking event and you see a man in a business suit who is the centre of attention. You also see a casually dressed woman sitting alone in a table. As you observe these two people, you immediately start inventing stories about their lives and applying labels to both based on preconceived ideas. Subconsciously, you are filling the gaps left in the limited pictures you're perceiving with information you have already learned. When you are not aware of this process, your objectivity may be impaired, and your interaction with the two people will be based on your biased, possibly erroneous thinking.

We are continually creating ideas and giving meaning to situations based on incomplete information that we observe. We make predictions and assumptions, but they may impair our ability to see the complete picture. We take our mental definitions as fact when, actually, they are coming from the limitations imposed by our conditioning. We develop opinions, and in doing so we are prevented from having an unbiased, objective view of a situation.

You open yourself to possibilities when you begin questioning your assumptions and considering situations from different perspectives.

SELECTIVE ATTENTION

Have you ever noticed that once you have decided to buy something, suddenly you see it everywhere? It was there all the time, but it was not until you thought about it that you began noticing it. That is an example of your selective attention at work.

Your brain is always selecting your focus. You didn't see the item before because your mind was not focused on it. Afterwards, when you decided to buy it, the item was in your awareness, your mind was directed and looked for it, and you saw it everywhere.

Your brain interacts similarly with your psychology. Your mind is always subconsciously looking for situations that will confirm your ingrained needs, your deep-rooted beliefs. But because your focus is not directed and you are not always aware of your conditioning, you are limiting yourself by only looking to confirm your current beliefs, ideas, and biases. Your selective attention is taking you on the same path that you were on before, and if you continue directing your life from the same conditioned framework, you will probably obtain the same results. The keys to breaking this cycle are to raise your consciousness, to become more self-aware, to increase your self-knowledge, and to focus on the present.

REWARDS

Similar to your brain's protection system that seeks to avoid pain is its reward system that prompts you to approach certain things with the expectation of pleasure. These two systems of the brain have evolved for your survival and self-preservation.

Two brain processes support your reward mechanism. The first one is the release of dopamine, a neurotransmitter that motivates you to take action to obtain what you anticipate will give you pleasure. Dopamine creates the desire, and it urges you to automatically act upon that desire. In other words, if your brain believes that something from your surroundings or something learned from your previous experiences will provide you with pleasure, you will start craving it and seek to obtain the reward— even if it is detrimental to your long-term health and well-being.

For example, imagine that to improve your health you have recently chosen a diet rich in vegetables. You go to a party where chocolate cake a dessert you have loved to eat countless times in the past and that you now associate with pleasure, is being served. When you see the cake, dopamine is released, causing you to crave it, and you find yourself reaching for it. Your brain has urged you to seek short-term pleasure rather than support your long-term goal. If you find yourself eating the whole cake instead of just a small piece, it is your dopamine at work. It creates a loop of cravings that is not satisfied until you become aware of the craving. Only then do you have the means to stop it.

When you have a craving, your brain works to figure out a way to satisfy it. It provides you with the reinforcement and excuses to satisfy that craving. For instance, in the prior example of the cake, your brain automatically will have provided you with thoughts such as, "I've been so good the past week," "I'm celebrating my friend's birthday," "Tomorrow I'll go to the gym," or "I'll only have one piece." You then acted upon the craving without questioning your thoughts.

This instant gratification focuses only on immediate pleasure. The pull of instant gratification also causes you to cling to past pleasurable experiences and makes you suffer when your current experience fails to match your past experience. Subconsciously, under the influence of this reward system, your brain is encouraging you to believe that recreating past pleasurable experiences is the only way to obtain satisfaction, and thus you create expectations based on those experiences. If those expectations are not met, you will feel upset or disappointed.

The second process of the reward mechanism is triggered by the release of other feel-good neurochemicals such as serotonin, endorphins, and oxytocin. These neurochemicals help you learn new behaviours, regulate your mood, feel pleasure, reduce pain, and create bonding. They are responsible for the "runner's high," among other things. For instance, think about the pleasure that you feel when you receive recognition, when you achieve a goal, when someone hugs you, or when you are kissing your loved one. That pleasant feeling you experience originates in this part of your reward system.

Your reward system also manifests itself when someone validates your beliefs, your feelings, your physical appearance, or your accomplishments. The good feeling you get further reinforces your behaviour. This becomes even more apparent when dealing with people you respect. This craving for validation can cause you to act against your best interests and values and instead seek short-term gratification.

In this way, your reward system can perpetuate bad habits and support those that don't add value to your life. Research suggests that it is linked to the creation of various addictions to alcohol, drugs, the internet, sex, gambling, shopping, or even work. It is helpful when you start recognizing precisely when your brain tempts you with instant gratification and when you're indulging in unsupportive behaviours. With that awareness, you can direct your thoughts, take action, and focus on long-term benefits.

* * *

In this part of the book you have learned, in a simplified way, about some very complex processes that your brain undergoes, and how these processes intrinsically influence your mindset, your thoughts, your conditioning, your behaviours, and your well-being. You are now empowered to be aware of your brain's influences and start choosing your thoughts and directing your behaviours. Through this conscious direction, you will be overriding the unconscious influence of your brain.

In the next part of the book, you will learn how you have been conditioned throughout your life. It is important to be aware of your conditioning so you can begin paying attention to the information you are exposing yourself to and how this conditioning triggers you.

You gain powerful insight from knowing how your mind has been trained. Based on this knowledge, you can create mental filters to discern between information that supports you and information that is potentially harmful.

— KEY SUMMARY POINTS —

1. Your brain and your mind are connected. Your brain's chemistry directly impacts your mood, and your mind's direction of your thoughts can alter that chemistry.

2. Your brain creates neural pathways for efficiency that are reinforced every time you repeat an action, feel the same emotion, or have the same thoughts.

3. With this repetition, these neural pathways become wider and more deeply entrenched in your subconscious mind, creating an efficient system for you to follow to direct your approach to life.

4. Your brain receives information from your environment through your senses, and then interprets this information using past knowledge and impressions that you have stored. Based on these interpretations, your brain constructs the world that you perceive and experience.

5. Our brains first evolved to protect us from physical harm. Today, our brains use the same mechanism to shelter us from psychological pain. In potentially threatening situations, your brain uses fear to cause you to react and protect yourself. However, that emotion prevents your mind from enjoying tranquility and peace.

6 Your brain provides meaning to anything you observe or experience, whether it is tangible or intangible. The meaning you give to intangible experiences comes from your conditioning. If your brain labels a situation as a threat, you will react to it with fear, but with deliberate thought you can override this reaction.

7 Circumstances don't have an intrinsic meaning. You define the meaning based on your interpretation and past experience. You can label circumstances consciously, or your brain will do it subconsciously. The event you experience is tagged in a memory that continues forming your conditioning.

8 To manage your psychological well-being, your brain prompts you to seek to control circumstances and other people's behaviours, even though in reality you only have control over yourself.

9 Neural pathways are patterns that allow you to operate automatically. These patterns support the growth and entrenchment of your physical or psychological habits. Although forming habits can be done consciously, it's most likely that you create your habits through subconscious repetition. Your habits determine the way you live.

10 You subconsciously create a negative bias toward present and future events, influenced by the brain's need to protect you. Without conscious thought, negative bias can spin you into a fearful cycle.

(11) The information you receive from your senses doesn't provide a full picture of what you are experiencing. Gaps remain that your brain fills with information assembled from your conditioning, and you thus build mental pictures and make decisions based on that incomplete information.

(12) Your brain is subconsciously directing your focus to confirm your beliefs and your notions about the world. If you have negative thoughts, negativity is all you see. If you believe there is lack, scarcity is all you see. Direct your focus to see what you wish to see.

(13) Your brain's release of dopamine incites you to approach something with expectations of pleasure but at the possible expense of your well-being.

PRACTICE SUGGESTIONS FOR PART 1

Following are some suggestions for practising conscious thinking. They will help you start using the power of your mind by directing it rather than allowing it to direct your life.

1 Start observing your mind.

Notice when your mind is drifting toward pessimistic thoughts. With that awareness, give direction to your mind.

- Direct your thoughts to look for possibilities and opportunities to grow.

- Consciously look for the positive aspects of the situation. What can you learn from it? What can you be grateful for?

- Think encouraging thoughts. It may feel awkward at first, but remember that you are reshaping your brain and creating new neural pathways. This takes conscious effort.

Benefit:

This exercise will help you to retrain your brain. You'll create habits of observing your mind, directing your thoughts, and seeing the potential and the positives in any given situation.

② Notice your cravings

Observe when you have a craving and the impulse or urge that it generates. With curiosity,

- Examine the gratification that you are seeking.

- Identify the benefits you will obtain by fulfilling your craving.

- Identify any negative consequences if you fulfill your craving.

- Assess whether giving in to your craving is contributing to your well-being.

③ Benefit:

This exercise will support you in harnessing the power of your mind and making intentional and positive choices.

Notice your judgments

Be aware of when:

- You are judging others from a first impression.

- You are inventing a story about a person's life based on their outward appearance.

- You are making assumptions about people's behaviours.

- You are making assumptions about situations.

- You are judging yourself.

Stop and realize that you are creating those ideas in your mind based on your conditioning. Become curious about other perspectives.

Benefit:

This exercise will help you uncover your biases, cultivate an open mindset, and train yourself to look for the larger picture.

4 Take occasional cold showers

I'm quite serious! Besides having health benefits, a cold shower can help you observe the nature of your mind. Notice the resistance of your mind and body when you are about to jump in, and then go for it. Notice how uncomfortable your body and mind feel in the cold water. Remain under the water for a few seconds without moving, and guide yourself to focus on your breathing. Relax into the cold—allow it, don't resist it. There is so much power in it.

Benefit:

This exercise will help you learn to feel at ease in uncomfortable circumstances, and to become more in tune within yourself.

PART TWO

YOUR MIND'S CONDITIONING

CHAPTER FIVE

HOW DID YOU BECOME CONDITIONED?

You can break yourself free from your hereditary patterns, cultural codes, social beliefs; and prove once and for all that the power within you is greater than the power that's in the world.
—Michael B. Beckwith

Throughout your life, you create concepts, ideas, and beliefs about the world. These ideas and beliefs are based on how you think you should behave, who you are supposed to be, how others should act, or how the world is supposed to evolve.

It began in childhood, when you looked to your parents and teachers as a source of knowledge. They taught you how to behave and what to believe in, and they shaped how you perceive the world and the meaning you give to your experiences. In adulthood, your friends, peers, and the media took over your parents' and teachers' roles. The process continues throughout your life, with both painful and joyful new experiences contributing to your store of memories. These memories create subconscious beliefs and ideas that define (and sometimes redefine) how you perceive yourself and the world. You are constantly being conditioned.

Think of these beliefs and ideas as programs that are running in your subconscious mind. The combination of all of them is your programming or personal conditioning. This programming is full of guiding beliefs that operate on autopilot as you are going about your life. As you are continually being influenced by external factors and personal experiences, you are programming and reprogramming your subconscious mind without your awareness or consent. You are continually placing new layers over old layers of beliefs that you use to interpret the world. And all these layers are blocking out the truth of who you are.

This programming is causing you to see and approach life with blinders. As you run the program repeatedly, you are narrowing your range of possibilities and limiting your ability to reach your highest potential, which prevents you from aligning with your purpose and connecting with your essence. This programming not only affects your well-being, but also impacts the well-being of others as you interact with them.

Until you become aware of your personal conditioning, you will continue living your life from your subconscious mind and on autopilot, recreating it from your past, obtaining the same results, and suffering unnecessarily.

In Part 3 you'll learn how to break free from your conditioning, but before we dive into that, it's essential to fully understand how your programming was first created so that you start recognizing and questioning your concepts, your beliefs, your ideas, your experiences, and how they impact you. It will be the first step to liberating yourself.

Let's look at the many ways you became conditioned.

Fear

The most significant conditioning factor in your life is fear. If you are not self-aware when you experience fear, it will incessantly drive your behaviours.

As I've said, it is important for you to remember how fear operates in your brain and how it impacts your mind. Your brain has evolved to protect you from harm and uses fear as your driving emotion. For instance, if you move to a new city, your brain could perceive it as psychological threat. Your conditioning will automatically want to protect you from the uncertainty of the unknown. To accomplish its purpose, your mind brings to your awareness all the risks and obstacles that you could potentially encounter with this new challenge. With all those negative and unsupportive thoughts in your mind, you start experiencing a series of emotions that all stem from fear, which causes you to avoid the unknown and stay put.

Fear manifests itself in your life through unpleasant emotions (like anger, for example), and when you take a close look at the root cause of them, you will likely find that you are protecting yourself from something.

Much like when you jump to the side to avoid the physical pain of being hit by a car, you will take a certain action or behave in a certain way to stop or to avoid the situation that will cause you psychological harm. For instance, you may be avoiding a challenging conversation because you are worried about the outcome. In the meantime, the lack of awareness keeps you dwelling on the situation, thus creating a vicious circle of worry and anxiety.

More examples of automatic subconscious reactions to fear are:

- Wanting to change someone's behaviours because they don't align with your conditioning

- Blaming others because you don't want to feel shame

- Not launching a project because you are afraid of failure

- Holding back your opinion in a meeting because you don't want to be embarrassed

- Staying in a bad relationship because you are afraid of being alone

Can you think of any of your own personal reactions to fear? Remember, you are yielding to fear when you are not conscious of how and where your fear manifests itself. In this mode, you will find yourself overreacting, seeking to control outside circumstances and becoming a victim of your subconscious emotions.

How fear conditions us

Fear can keep us imprisoned within the confines of our conditioning. It is often buried in our minds.

Through fear, we create certain beliefs, such as how we should be in the world and how others should behave. These beliefs are created when we directly experience life's painful episodes and also through external influences. We label all of them as painful in our minds, and they became ingrained as threats in our subconscious. We become conditioned by those beliefs and experiences.

Imagine that you have a painful experience that your brain records as a threat. When your brain perceives that it might happen again, your programming will react and seek to avoid it. For instance, one of my conditioned fears manifested itself in romantic relationships. After having my heart broken several times, I developed a belief that "being in a relationship is very painful." I recall the beginning of my relationship with an ex-boyfriend, when I felt strongly like running away. My mind was arguing that he was not the right person for me, and I even began to criticize him. Subconsciously, I was sabotaging the very relationship that my heart was desiring! By then, I was already doing the inner work, and I was aware of what was going on within me—I knew I was experiencing fear. With that awareness, I guided my mind through the process with love and compassion each time I noticed fear creeping up on me.

Fear also conditions you when you view your identity as set in stone. Here is an example: assume that throughout your adult life, you have always been in a relationship. You cannot conceive of yourself as being alone; the only way you know yourself is as a person with a partner. Thus your life experience has shaped a subconscious belief that "living alone is painful." The fear of being alone becomes the driving force in your life, so much so that you aren't flexible enough to see other possibilities.

Another way in which fear may be conditioning you is when others imprint you with their beliefs. For instance, you may believe that certain things are essential for you to be happy. Subconsciously, you are fearful of not having those things and you are willing to do almost anything to obtain them. But are you aware of where those beliefs are coming from?

Often, without even being aware of it, we give away our power—and our happiness—to people who tell us what *they* believe is required for us to be happy. They condition us, and we act based on those external beliefs, allowing them to dictate the terms of our happiness.

Fear is often used by others to control our behaviours and to influence how we approach life. For example, I heard about a sales manager who told his team, "You know what will happen if you don't make your sales quota." That statement acts as a psychological threat that will drive his team's behaviours. Using fear, he controls their activities by threatening their financial security. Fear is widely used to motivate us to do things when it is pointed out to us what we will likely lose or the pain we will experience if we don't do the thing in question.

Our society has been conditioned to operate in fear. If you take the time to observe your surroundings, you will notice that fear is everywhere. It shows up in trivial interactions—for instance, at work when people avoid speaking up because of fear of being judged or when advertising claims that your happiness depends on having this or that product.

Yet fear is created solely by you, in your mind. It creates beliefs that guide your life. Fear creates a cycle of suffering that affects not only your own well-being, but also that of millions of people around the world.

Now you are aware of how fear works. You've allowed your mind to create it, and you have the power to go beyond it as you become the master of your mind. You can learn how to go beyond fear by mastering your emotions, something we'll cover in Part 3. In the meantime, let's continue with your other conditioners.

Beliefs

Throughout your life you create beliefs. Whether they come from your life experiences or were taught by your parents, friends, teachers, or colleagues, these beliefs direct and guide your life. Some of your beliefs can be so trivial that they don't affect your day-to-day life, while others can cause you to make life-changing, irreversible decisions. Altogether, all the beliefs you hold form one major conditioning unit.

What is a belief? Let's define a belief as an idea or concept that you believe is true. It can be about yourself, intangible things, material goods, other people, or even the world.

There are empowering and disempowering beliefs. Empowering beliefs support you in your life. For instance, consider the belief that "everything happens for a reason." This belief will help you overcome setbacks, and see them as opportunities to learn and grow. Disempowering beliefs are those that limit you in some way, that are not serving you in a positive way. For example, "Bad things always happen to me." This belief can cause you to feel like a victim of life. It clearly does not support you in overcoming difficulties, as you are unlikely to seek out the learning opportunities that are hidden in your struggle.

Your mind reinforces your beliefs. This means that, whether you are aware of it or not, your mind is always looking for proof that your beliefs are real, and when it finds what it thinks is that proof, it reinforces those beliefs. That's why you often see things that validate what you believe, or you see what you expect to see.

For example, if you have a subconscious belief that "people don't take me seriously," you will react by not expressing your ideas or voicing your opinion, by not applying for a leadership position, or by not going to networking or social events. Now imagine that one day you bravely decided to approach a colleague to share your opinion, but you felt she dismissed you. The first thought that probably came to your mind was, "She didn't take my suggestion seriously." But what you might not have considered is that perhaps she was in a hurry for another meeting, or perhaps she wasn't feeling well. You automatically assumed that the perceived rejection was about you, and now you are taking her response personally. Your subconscious mind is confirming the belief that people don't take you seriously. This experience further confirms your belief system and your victimization of yourself.

But how true is this belief to you? And where did it come from? Did one of your parents pass it on to you? Or maybe someone made fun of your ideas in high school?

This happens to everyone. We go through life creating beliefs and ideas about everything we experience and everyone we meet. We are continually being influenced by external factors that shape our belief system, and yet we have not been taught how to look within to discern how true those beliefs really are to us.

One of my beliefs was that "women cannot be beautiful and smart at the same time." When I finally realized it, I saw scenes of my life flash through my mind's eye, and only then did I understand my behaviours at different stages of my life.

In high school in my native Colombia, I was part of the nerdy group; I was smart and had high marks. At the same time, I didn't think I was beautiful, because subconsciously I believed that it was not possible to be both beautiful and smart at the same time.

At university, I began taking care of my appearance by dressing up, doing my hair, and using makeup to acknowledge my beauty. But it didn't change my belief, because now that I considered myself to be beautiful, I started thinking I was not smart! That, too, drove my behaviours. Although my opinion of myself changed, my unconscious belief stayed the same.

Fast-forward to Canada, where my behaviours continued to be guided by that subconscious belief. At work, I dressed in suits, put my hair back in a ponytail, and cut back on makeup. I remember thinking that I didn't want people to think that I was beautiful. Unknowingly, I was driven by my belief to downplay my appearance, since being smart was essential to my new career.

I spent years working in the corporate world and continuing to grow as a woman in a male-dominated industry. To advance in my career, I was always seeking to learn from other women leaders. In one book written by a woman, I recall reading something like, "Own your beauty." "Yes!" I told myself. "That's what I am going to do." I started owning my beauty. But again I began feeling that

I was not smart—I noticed it in my interactions and behaviours.

This time, however, I was already doing the inner work of paying attention to my thoughts. I quickly became aware of the conditioned self-talk that was telling me I was not smart. With that awareness, I started to rewire my brain by telling myself, "I am smart *and* beautiful." I repeated this often, to the extent that I would correct men when they told me I was beautiful by adding, "And I'm smart too."

Rewiring my brain with this affirmation not only helped me to feel smart, but also improved my confidence at work—all while owning my beauty. But this approach was only a temporary solution—a deep, conditioned belief was still driving my behaviours. It came up again when, as a sales account manager, one of my tasks was to build trusting relationships with senior leaders of the companies that were part of my accounts. I remember hesitating when I was about to make a call. The voice in my head would tell me, "They won't believe you're smart." The belief was so strong that even though they had never met or seen me, I was still grappling with the emotion created by the belief that I could not be both smart and beautiful.

I was thankful for the fact that I was already carrying out the inner work necessary to understand my emotions, to discover my personal conditioning and belief system. It was fascinating to observe how that belief had directed my life for so many years, guiding my behaviours in limiting ways, and ultimately eroding my self-confidence and self-worth. When I became conscious of my belief, I began to see that it was not true to who I was. It felt as if a heavy weight was lifted from my shoulders.

Different people will give different meanings to similar experiences. For example, my belief was set at a young age while watching beauty contests in Colombia and hearing comments (on TV as well as from my family) such as, "Of course she's not smart, because she's beautiful." Yet my sister, who is only few years younger and was exposed to the same experiences, grew up with an entirely different belief: "Women can be smart and beautiful."

My experience with this belief highlights very clearly how our minds, working on autopilot, can direct our lives. Can you see now how your belief system may be affecting you? My inner work also revealed a number of other limiting beliefs I had been harbouring, but the one I've shared here had the most impact on my career.

I trust this section has shown you how you can be trapped by your beliefs and has empowered you to pay attention to what you are telling yourself, to start challenging your self-created ideas and understand where they are coming from. With conscious effort, you will be able to see your conditioned beliefs for what they are—simply concepts formed and stuck in your mind, whether they are true or false.

Life experiences

Every single life experience you've had has been added to your conditioning. This conditioning began when you were born, and if you don't consciously interfere, it continues building throughout your life. The experiences that had the most significant emotional impact on you are those that have most strongly influenced your inner programming.

Let's say that in a team project in high school, you suggested an idea to your teammates with which they didn't agree and for which they made fun of you. Your brain stored this experience with a seed of belief that "my ideas don't matter, so why even bother expressing them?" Perhaps this became a pattern that repeated itself in different school situations. Now fast-forward to the workplace: in your first job, in a meeting, you gave an idea, and everyone looked at you disapprovingly, completely ignoring your comment.

Those cumulative experiences served only to reinforce your belief.

Your mind will attempt to protect you by preventing you from sharing your ideas at work, withholding your thoughts for fear of being judged unworthy, and ultimately impacting the communication between you and your colleagues and loved ones.

Knowing all of this, can you imagine how many experiences you've had in your lifetime that created false beliefs about you and about the world? How long have you been confining yourself inside your subconscious mind to protect yourself from emotional pain?

Family

When you were growing up, your family was your first source of information for how to interpret the world. Your family influenced your choice of activities, friendships, study, relationships, career, and your relationship to the world in general.

Your parents may also have passed on to you their own fears. While they may have sought to protect you from pain, this protection could be hampering your resilience and your creativity in life.

Here's an example from my past. As a child, I recall that my parents had enough money to live a comfortable life in Bogotá. Their business was going very well until, through a series of unfortunate circumstances, it collapsed. I was about seventeen years old when my parents went bankrupt. I remember that it was a tough time for my parents, but now, as an adult, I can also recognize the impact it had in my life.

It was then that my father taught me that "you can lose everything, but no one can take away what you have learned and experienced." That belief shaped my life, instilling in me a lifelong passion for learning and for having experiences.

But if I learned that knowledge and experiences are to be greatly valued, during that difficult time I also learned that money can be scarce, and for years afterwards, I managed my money carefully—at least I thought I did. For many years I kept putting my money in the bank, where it earned a paltry interest rate, rather than investing it. The concept of investing seemed far too scary. I even bought a car with a loan, paying interest rates, although I had enough saved to pay for the car in full! Seeing my money in the bank gave me a perceived sense of safety.

It was later in my life, through a mentor whose belief was that "money comes easily and frequently," that I began understanding more about how money works and the fear-based relationship I had with it. My new-found awareness helped me to retrain my brain with a new belief, but it was not until I started to look within me and bring to light the origin of my conditioning that I understood my dysfunctional relationship with money.

Your parents taught you in the best way they knew, and they likely did the best they could with their knowledge and resources at the time. But with that close association between parents and child comes a deep set of beliefs that needs to be re-examined in adulthood.

Social circles

Humans are social creatures, so it is fundamentally important to our health and well-being to be part of a community and to have relationships. We rely on our social circles for support and to provide us with a sense of self-worth and belonging. When our friends and colleagues share their beliefs and values with us, often they can confirm and further condition our own.

For instance, if you are part of a social circle that believes in healthy eating and exercising, you will probably develop a new set of beliefs or reinforce the beliefs that you already hold regarding a healthy lifestyle. Similarly, if you belong to a group of people who like to drink and party, you may feel validated if you share those behaviours.

Your social circles influence what you believe in, how you behave, who you are, and how you relate to others. If you are unaware of this influence, you might act in ways that are not true to you simply because you want to fit in.

Throughout different stages of your life, your social circles and relationships will likely change, yet each of those past relationships will have shaped your conditioning.

When you start consciously observing your social circles, you will begin to understand how you have been influenced and how they have shaped the way you think, your beliefs, and your values. When you choose your social circles and relationships, choose wisely, because they have a very strong influence on you.

The media

Media in all its forms can substantially influence your belief system. Newspapers, magazines, radio, television, and the internet— in particular, advertising—all influence your choices regarding your appearance, your behaviour, and your material possessions. They even affect the meaning you assign to things, places, and people.

Digital media, through the gathering of your personal information, can more precisely target you. Without your critical thinking and awareness, the internet can overly influence your tendencies and your beliefs, and therefore drive your behaviours.

Simply becoming aware of the media's influence will prevent you from allowing others to imprint their ideas and impose their agendas on you.

Culture

I am grateful that, having lived in three different countries on three continents, I have been exposed to different cultures. It has helped me to see first-hand how the diversity of the belief and value systems of each country has shaped their citizens' lives.

Your set of beliefs was largely developed by the surroundings you grew up in. For instance, if you were born in a part of India where eating meat goes against the beliefs and customs, you probably grew up vegetarian. If you then travelled to places like Argentina where it is culturally acceptable to eat beef, you would still be looking for a vegetarian restaurant because it is part of your cultural makeup. You wouldn't need to think twice.

Your behaviour is similar regarding the way you think. For example, let's imagine that you grew up and are now working in a country where women are not often viewed as leaders. Since you grew up with this reference and your society has the same attitude, this belief that it is not possible for women to be leaders has conditioned you. It has programmed you and the people around you, including most women. If you are a woman, this belief will likely guide your behaviours and aspirations. If you are a man, unconsciously you may be imposing this belief on the women in your life, thus limiting their potential.

In addition, societal rules that have been created throughout history often dictate what is expected from you. These rules serve a purpose, setting common ground for an orderly and harmonious society. But if you comply unconsciously with these rules, you may be preventing yourself from exploring other possibilities in your society.

Education

Your education has a tremendous influence on your fundamental way of thinking. Your educational choices dictate the way you perceive the world.

For example, an artist sees the world differently from an engineer. It would be difficult for an artist to perceive the world from an engineer's perspective and vice versa. Their different perspectives obviously serve a purpose for their professions, but they also shape a way of thinking that influences other aspects of their lives.

It's important to notice when your education may be getting in your way. You can start by paying attention to times when you find yourself stubbornly clinging to an old idea, blocking a new idea, or being unable to see another's point of view.

Work experience

Work experiences define you through the knowledge you gain, the title you have, or the role you play.

Have you ever noticed co-workers who seem set in their ways, and unaware of it? They continue doing the same things over and over, unaware that they are trapped in the box their work experience has put them in. They are not flexible about changing their methods of working because that is all they know.

The way you interact with your managers and your mentors sets the direction for how you accomplish your job. You learn through them, ask them for advice, and observe how they behave in various situations. This supports you in your career and your growth, adds value to your work experience, and makes you more efficient and effective. But limitations are created if you inherit some of their beliefs and attitudes that don't support or contribute to your career. Any negative conditioning you adopt at work can not only impact your work, but also your personal life.

This happened with one of my clients. As we worked on his leadership style and explored the approaches he wished to take with his team, we discovered that, subconsciously, his management style was based on what he had inherited from his own managers. He didn't know any other way of functioning, and his conditioned behaviour was preventing him from connecting and building trust with his team.

Conditioned fear could also be affecting your experiences at work and your attitude toward your work. You may be behaving and making decisions based on protecting your position rather than following your instinctive wisdom and being authentic.

Values and what *you* value

Values are the principles by which you live. They are your drivers. They highlight what is important to you, what you hold most dear in your life. Throughout your life, you've created new values and left others behind. You can consciously create your values or let them evolve as your circumstances change. You are driven by your values, factoring them into any decisions you make.

Subconsciously, you also assign value to things, events, and relationships and therefore give them meaning. You create a narrative about the situation, and you become trapped in that narrow meaning to the exclusion of others.

For instance, I was suffering because I was holding onto the idea that being in a romantic relationship was more valuable than any other type of relationship. But who's to say which kind of relationship is more valuable? Well, I did. I subconsciously created that idea, but all it did was cause me pain. When I finally became aware of my conditioned thinking, I chose to allow my relationship to transform itself into what it was meant to be rather than limit it to a single label. I chose to accept it and appreciate it for what it was. Coming to this realization and deliberately directing my thoughts allowed me to find peace.

Many people also subconsciously create fear-based values. If you recall our discussion on fear, you can see that fear-based values arise because your mind is looking to protect you in some way. The best way to explain this is with an example. Imagine that you value accuracy so much that it sometimes takes you longer than others to get things done. You may ask yourself, "Why am I this way?" If you dig deep into your memories, you may find that your brain is protecting you from the pain you once encountered at university when a paper you wrote was not precise and detailed enough for a passing grade, and from that day on, you began to value accuracy so that the experience would not repeat itself. Subconsciously, you have been living your life according to this fear-based value. You were conditioned.

On the other hand, you've created other values that bring you joy and light your heart. Perhaps you value learning; thus, you feel fulfilled anytime you read or take a workshop or do anything to express this value.

Unknowingly, you may have conflicting values, as one of my clients did when she was looking for a new job. She valued both challenge and safety. The challenge value was pulling her forward to go after a new career, but the safety value was holding her back from stepping outside her comfort zone. Her lack of awareness about these conflicting values was making her feel uneasy, stressed, and frustrated. These two values were directing her behaviour, keeping her "spinning the wheels" of her life.

Start recognizing what your values are, what you deem important in your life, and what values you assign to various circumstances; once you do this, you are sure to find inner peace.

Habits

A habit is something you do frequently enough that it becomes a deep-seated behaviour. If you take a moment and look at your daily life, you will notice that it is made up of habits. They are programs that are ingrained in the neural pathways of your brain. You may have created them because of your life circumstances, because that was all you knew, or because you picked them up from others. They are dictating the direction of your life and how you experience it.

When I was doing inner work on myself, I decided to take a deeper look into the areas that were essential for my well-being. When I realized that I had unhealthy eating habits and didn't know much about nutrition, I decided to change. It took a conscious effort to modify my unhealthy behaviours around food, but after a time I was able to achieve a healthier lifestyle. I decided to choose new values to support the creation of my new, healthier habit, and I created a new belief that by eating healthily I was showing myself love.

Habits allow you to perform tasks without thinking about them. Once you become aware of them, you can choose to reinforce or transform them to suit your needs. Work on bringing awareness to your habits and recognizing the patterns you exhibit so you can choose the ones that benefit you. In the bonus section of Part 3, you will learn how to change a habit so that you are no longer a slave to your unsupportive or destructive ones.

* * *

Until this point, we've been discussing how you have been conditioned throughout your life. You know the factors that are constantly influencing you and have programmed your mind. You can now observe your behaviours, pay attention to your thoughts, become curious about your beliefs, and choose your habits. You can use the information you have gathered from your self-observation through this chapter to grow in self-awareness and evolve in self-knowledge. You can now decide to let go of the subconscious influences of your mind and the automatic reactions that come from your programming.

In the next chapter, we will delve into a discussion about ego—what it is, and how it manifests itself in your life.

— KEY SUMMARY POINTS —

1 You create beliefs about yourself, others, and the world. Those beliefs form the foundation of your conditioning, acting as programs you use to approach life. Operating from this framework limits you to the constraints of your conditioning and causes you to live on autopilot.

2 The protection mechanism of your brain conditions you to react fearfully in unfamiliar and undesirable situations, allowing fear to control your thoughts and behaviours. As you learn to master your mind, you can go beyond fear.

3 Your painful life experiences have created beliefs and memories that your brain perceives as threats. These threats become rooted in your subconscious mind and, over time, become your conditioning.

4 The experiences that have most deeply impacted you on an emotional level are those that shape your belief system.

5 A lack of awareness of your conditioning and its influence may be sabotaging and misdirecting your life. Uncover your conditioning and free yourself from these self-imposed limitations.

6 Different influences have shaped your conditioning, and they continue to program and reprogram it. Some of those conditioners are:

- *Fear:* Fear prevents you from surpassing your limitations and getting out of your comfort zone.

- *Your family:* Your first source of information, your family provides you with the original framework from which to navigate your life.

- *Your social circle:* Your friends can create and reinforce your beliefs thorough their strong influence.

- *The media:* TV, movies, the internet, and other media strongly influence what you like, who you think you should be, and what you think you should have.

- *Your culture:* Different cultures generate different, specific sets of beliefs and values.

- *Your education:* Your educational background has created a framework of thinking that applies to your work and to other areas of your life.

- *Your work experience:* You inherit habits, beliefs, and behaviours from your colleagues and your work environment.

- *Your values and what you value:* You make decisions in life based on your values. When you give meaning to something, you assign it value, which becomes the basis for your behaviours.

- *Your habits:* Your habits act as programs that run your life. Your lack of awareness of them is conditioning you and likely limiting you in certain ways.

CHAPTER SIX

THE EGO

Ego is just like dust in the eyes.
Without clearing the dust,
we can't see anything clearly,
so clear the ego and see the world.
—Anonymous

Ego, the sense of self, the sense of "I" as a unique being, is an intrinsic part of being human. Ego is how you identify with yourself. It is the identity or identities that you have created for who you believe you are. It is how you perceive yourself to be and how you identify with that perception. It allows you to differentiate yourself from others. In this sense, ego allows you to experience your humanity.

Throughout each stage of your life, your ego constructs not just one identity, but multiple identities that have defined you. In this way, ego supports you to navigate different aspects of your life, wherever it determines a need. The downside of ego occurs when you allow it, most often unconsciously, to take over. That's when things can get out of control. But rejecting or fighting your ego means rejecting a part of yourself. What's key is understanding your ego, keeping it in check, and not allowing it to control you.

Instead, with your awareness, you want to guide it.

In many cases, the ego's identities dictate your behaviours so you can live in agreement with who you perceive you are. These perceptions of yourself also help create your belief system, which includes a blueprint for how you should behave in various circumstances, who you should be, and what you should have.

Your ego helps you navigate both your personal and professional life, influencing how you interact with others, as well as your role in your family, in your work, and in society. Ego also tells you what you perceive should be yours and what is important to you or not: your house, car, other possessions, degree, partner, money, beliefs, ideas, job, title, social status, and so on.

Each of us has an ego. The questions are: Is your ego controlling your life without you knowing about it? And if so, what are the consequences of allowing your ego to direct your life?

Your ego identities come with a set of values, beliefs, rules, and expectations. Besides creating a subconscious narrative about who you are, what you do, how your life should be, and what things you should have, ego also has expectations for how others should be and behave toward you.

To use an analogy, ego functions much like a job description. It has a list of rules and expectations that you must meet to satisfy it. This narrative of your ego has been created through your personal conditioning and influenced by others during your upbringing and life experiences.

You might be so attached to your ego identities that you must perform according to them, behaving by their rules; otherwise you might find yourself in disagreement with what you believe you are. If you occasionally find yourself thinking, "I don't feel like myself" or "I don't know what I would do with my life if [fill in the blank]," it's because you are not in compliance with the identity of your ego. You expect to maintain the status quo, but when you find yourself outside of the prescribed boundaries set by your ego or when your ego is challenged, it becomes frightened and wants to protect itself. It strives to protect its identities and all the ideas, beliefs, and behaviours that are in accordance with them. When you strongly identify with your ego, subconsciously you are measuring your self-worth and your value against those ego identities.

Ego can keep you living in fear. If someone, something, or some situation jeopardizes any of your identities by affecting your image, by rejecting one of your beliefs, or by threatening your property, your ego will become defensive. It will cause you to feel unpleasant emotions, which in turn will drive you to react negatively to these psychological threats. Thus it helps you understand how your ego, with its insistence on being inflexible about its expectations, rules and needs, prevents you from seeing what is possible for you.

The best way to further explain ego is with an example. Imagine that you are a famous athlete. Your whole life has revolved around your sport. You awaken early to train, participate in competitions on the weekends, and befriend only those who share your interest. You build a career as an athlete, playing in the big leagues, getting sponsorships, making lots of money to buy a big house, a fancy car, and a lavish lifestyle. You have arrived. You say to yourself, "I am an athlete." It's your entire identity.

Then abruptly, due to an injury, your career is over. You feel lost. You don't know what to do with your life because your ego still believes that you are an athlete, but your situation is not satisfying the demands of your ego.

You feel you would do anything to have your career back. You are upset, blaming everything and everyone for your injury, feeling confused, frustrated, and worried. You are suffering. What are you going to do with your life without sports? Who are you now? How do you define yourself? You have known yourself only as an athlete and your self-worth was based on that. This identity had run your entire life till the moment that ended your career. You lived based on the belief that being an athlete defined you.

And now that your identity has been taken away from you, your ego feels threatened. You have been forced to realize that your old identity can no longer define you and you must move forward with your life. It is (and always has been) your choice to free yourself from any identity or identities you have fashioned for yourself that dictate and influence the decisions you make daily.

Another example relates to my decision to improve my well-being by creating healthy lifestyle habits. I began exercising regularly and chose a healthier diet. It took perseverance, but after a few years of embodying my new habits, subconsciously I created a new identity for myself of a healthy, athletic person. Even so, this new identity had rules that I had to comply with if I were to live my life based on that specific identity. Then one day I suffered a cycling injury that prevented me from training for months. Since my athletic identity required me to exercise a minimum of six times a week, I could no longer be true to that identity, and as a result I began to suffer. Since I was not yet aware of my ego identity, I felt very frustrated and upset with myself during my recovery.

Through self-examination, using the emotions I was experiencing, this injury helped me to discover my ego's identity. I recognized that my ego had been so focused on being athletic that it had prevented me from enjoying nature while exercising. It also made me feel guilty when I ate unhealthily, and it caused further conflict with others because I had been subconsciously imposing on them the beliefs and values associated with my identity as a healthy, athletic person.

Although this identity was a positive one that contributed to my well-being, I was not aware of the other areas in which my ego was limiting me. This realization empowered me to make new, conscious choices, ones that allowed me to *truly* enjoy healthy living. I learned to accept people for who they are and not label them with what I wanted them to be. Now, instead of imposing my way of life on others, I choose to respect the fact that their lifestyle is their choice to make, not mine.

When you are not self-aware, every decision you make, whether a big one that requires more consideration or small ones that you make daily, contributes to satisfying your ego. Without self-awareness, when you buy a house or car or when you speak in a meeting or talk to your partner, you are doing so to satisfy the requirements of your ego. When a decision is between two or more unpleasant options, you'll choose the option that least harms your ego.

Recognize those times when your ego manifests itself, when it is making decisions to satisfy its needs, and when it is making you suffer as it seeks to comply with its identities. That awareness can help you start taking ownership and responsibility for the direction of your life.

Two ways to become aware of the identities you have created are through an examination of your unpleasant emotions, and through consciously observing your thoughts and behaviours (you will learn how in Part 3 of this book).

Another way is to notice those times when your ego manifests itself and work on understanding how it operates. Following are some examples of how ego manifests itself. Once you know these, you can be more prepared for them, and you can start directing your ego instead of letting it direct you.

EGO LIKES TO LOOK GOOD

This is one of ego's favourites. Ego enjoys impressing others and showing off. This manifestation of ego prevents you from displaying your authentic self and impairs collaboration with others. As a result, you'll have difficulty connecting and creating trusting relationships.

Ego makes you believe you are better than others, creating separation between you and the world. It prevents you from being kind, empathetic, and compassionate toward others and from putting yourself in their shoes. Your ego will look down on others in order to boost itself.

Since ego enjoys looking good, it finds it challenging to ask for help, to receive any feedback, or to recognize its blind spots. As humans, we learn by experimenting, by trial and error, and by making mistakes. But ego does not like accepting mistakes or failure, and finds ways to blame others for these. Ego's belief that it knows everything is keeping you restricted in your growth and evolution.

EGO PROTECTS ITS SELF-IMAGE

Your ego is looking to defend the image it has created. It leaves you closed-minded to other perspectives and keeps you from seeing opportunities.

When you are not complying with your ego's image of you, when you are not behaving in your usual conditioned way, your ego will express the disagreement between how it thinks you are supposed to behave and how you are actually behaving. This disagreement manifests itself through unpleasant emotions such as guilt and frustration. The discord between your ego-created image and your new behaviours can prevent you from experiencing a greater enjoyment in your life and seeing more possibilities for yourself.

Your ego sometimes casts you in the role of a victim. You blame others and outside circumstances so you can avoid taking responsibility and protect your ego's polished, perfect image. Your ego then creates a screen, preventing you from seeing what is really occurring and consequently from taking steps to overcome your undesirable circumstances.

EGO LOOKS FOR ACCEPTANCE

In its search for approval, your ego may diminish you in order for you to fit in and be liked by your peers.

When your ego seeks acceptance, it will compromise its own set of beliefs in order to embrace the beliefs of those from whom it craves acceptance. As a result, you find yourself downplaying your achievements and accomplishments, and not speaking your mind regarding something you truly believe in. You are acting on fear of disapproval. Perhaps the worst part of not being true to yourself is that your confidence and self-worth gradually become eroded.

EGO WANTS TO BE RIGHT

Have you ever noticed how good you feel when someone tells you that you are right? How it feels even better to have gained the upper hand by winning a long argument? That is your ego at work.

When you assume the attitude of "I have to be right," you shut yourself down from understanding different points of view, compromising, and achieving resolutions. Your ego's need to be right also impacts your relationships by making you argumentative and dismissive of others' perspectives.

Your performance at work and in life will almost certainly be negatively affected by this constant need. It prevents you from having an open mind, learning from others, and from creating trusting relationships.

EGO SEEKS VALIDATION OF ITS OWN IDENTITY OR IDENTITIES

Your ego looks for others to validate its identity, which includes your perspectives, behaviours, intelligence, decisions, possessions, and the work you do. It creates conflict by rallying others to support its opinion, which can result in friction between you and the person(s) from whom you seek validation.

Ego doesn't like to be judged by others; it craves the opposite, which is validation. If it doesn't get this, internal conflict is created, and you start having self-doubts and feeling anxious and worried, which affects your self-confidence. Your ego will do anything to gain validation from others. Ego can tie up your entire self-worth in other people's opinions.

EGO BELIEVES THAT ITS WAY IS THE ONLY WAY

This is another of your ego's favourites, and it is a function of ego's need to be right. Ego believes—sometimes secretly—that the only way to do something is its own way, based on its own identity. When it is not trying to fit in and be accepted, ego can go in the opposite direction, imposing its own beliefs and values on others and trying to dictate how they should behave. This too is a form of ego validation.

Ego's fear-driven agenda pushes its "my way or the highway" approach because of its need to be right. In its insecurity, ego can't bear to be wrong. It negatively affects your engagement, connection, and collaboration with other people, ultimately breaking down trust. In extreme cases, ego's need to change others' beliefs and ways of behaving to conform to its own ways can result in harmful bullying.

EGO CREATES PERCEPTIONS AND ASSUMPTIONS

Ego has a bias right out of the gate about how things are supposed to be. These biased assumptions stem from how you perceive yourself. Because of ego's assumptions, your opportunity to grow and learn something new is restricted.

Your ego is always looking to confirm its identity. If you continue approaching your life from the same perceptions and assumptions, you keep your ego very happy indeed, but at the price of your potential and your relationships.

EGO CREATES EXPECTATIONS

Ego is always creating expectations of how things are supposed to be, how others are supposed to behave, and how things are supposed to look, according to it. When these expectations are not fulfilled, your ego will try to manipulate and control the circumstances to fit the requirements of its desired outcome.

Whether or not your ego's expectations are met, your perspective remains stubbornly limited, and you miss opportunities to learn from the situation. You may suffer from emotional pain, your relationships may be hindered, and worst of all, your authentic self may become even more deeply buried.

EGO LOVES CONTROL

Ego does not like uncertainty. It feels uncomfortable with the unknown and any change. It wants to control outcomes, situations, and people.

The only constant in the world around you is change. You can't control outside circumstances, other people's behaviours, attitudes, or desires, the economy, world events, and so on. Yet your ego seeks to control them, ostensibly to protect itself, which it does by resisting them. Because of that resistance, you suffer—you become upset, frustrated, sad, depressed, or enraged—and you feel overwhelmingly helpless. But when you consciously work to disable your ego, you'll begin to understand that the only thing you can control is your own mind.

Ego's control and its resistance to change can preclude you from discovering other possibilities because it forces you to focus on controlling outcomes rather than seeing the opportunities that come with change. Those missed opportunities could enhance your life in ways that you might never imagine.

EGO CREATES SEPARATION

Ego is solely focused on me, myself, and I, and it therefore safeguards anything in its belief system to the exclusion of others' beliefs. Opposing others' beliefs and values without trying to understand, accept, and respect them as another way of living often causes wide gulfs of separation among people. This defence mechanism is based on fear that the ego will lose its identity or identities and its need to always be right.

This kind of ego-driven separation is causing a vast amount of suffering in our world. In the process of protecting itself, the ego damages relationships, breaks up families, and interferes with productive collaboration. It causes arguments, fights, and even wars because it prevents people from working together for the common good of society and from taking care of one another, of the environment, and of the world. One only needs to observe the egos of certain politicians to see how damaging they can be to citizens' harmony with others and with nature.

Ego gets in the way of respecting each other's values, perspectives, beliefs, and cultures. Conflict arises when people are not aware that they are being controlled by their egos. They erroneously believe that they are in control of their lives when in fact the opposite is true.

Perhaps somewhat ironically, ego is inescapable; it is a necessary part of being human. The solution is not to seek to eliminate it, but rather to recognize that it exists and to acknowledge how it influences you so you can consciously guide your mind away from its unsupportive characteristics and mechanisms of control. With this knowledge, you are empowered to live your life with a conscious awareness of your ego, thus freeing you from the demands that it subconsciously imposes on you and your identification with it.

* * *

As a society, we have been conditioned to believe that power is outside of ourselves, that it is based on having material possessions, money, a high social status, an important title, a leadership position, and so on. Perhaps you don't see yourself as a powerful person because you don't have these things that society values, but these things don't bestow true power. In reality, true power comes from within. Your *inner power*, when used for good, can make you a powerful human being who can create change. This power comes when both the subconscious images you have created about yourself *and* your personal conditioning are no longer controlling the way you live, when you have consciously chosen how to direct your life from your essence and not from your mental creations. When you access your true power, you start responding to life organically, allowing it to unfold with ease and flow. You achieve *inner peace* because you are not emotionally battered by life's circumstances or by other's people behaviours. You have freed yourself from your defined identities, from your limiting beliefs, from deriving your worth from others' opinions, and from being a slave to the material world. When you step into your true power, you free yourself from your ego's control, you find real purpose, and you start living authentically.

It is your choice to give yourself the most essential and beautiful gift in your life—the gift of freedom from your conditioned mind and your ego's control—and step into your true power. You give it to yourself by doing the inner work to reveal your autopilot programming, by exposing the ego's identities that have dictated your life, and by aligning to your true essence, your soul.

* * *

In Part 3, we will delve into how to get out of your conditioned mind and uncover the self-created programming and identities that have been ruling your life and that have limited you from living fully and in peace.

— KEY SUMMARY POINTS —

(1) Ego is the identity or identities through which you define and perceive yourself. It is what you believe you are, who you think you should be, what you think you're supposed to have, and how you think you're supposed to behave.

(2) Your ego has beliefs that further form the foundation of your conditioning. Your lack of awareness of those beliefs is, ironically, keeping you living according to them.

(3) Your ego's identities come with narratives that describe how you should live and what behaviours you expect from yourself and others. Behaviours that do not comply with these narratives cause you emotional pain.

(4) Ego keeps you living in fear, affecting your mental and physical well-being. It can control your life.

(5) The awareness that comes from recognizing your ego is very empowering. With this awareness, you can step into your true power and begin to take responsibility for and ownership of your life.

(6) Managing your ego is not about getting rid of it; rather, it is about supporting your human experience. It is about recognizing your ego and not allowing it to take control over your life with its needs and expectations.

(7) You can uncover your ego in three ways—by observing your thoughts and behaviours, through self-examination, and by recognizing when ego shows up in your life.
Your ego can manifest itself in these ways:

- Ego likes to look good.

- Ego protects its self-image.

- Ego looks for acceptance.

- Ego wants to be right.

- Ego seeks validation of its own identity or identities.

- Ego believes that its way is the only way.

- Ego creates perceptions and assumptions.

- Ego creates expectations.

- Ego loves control.

- Ego creates separation.

PRACTICE SUGGESTIONS FOR PART 2

1 Observe your ego

Begin to notice times when you want to be right or you want to impose your point of view. You can use your interactions at work, with your partner, or with family and friends. When you notice this impulse:

- Step 1: Stop.

- Step 2: Notice your defensiveness.

- Step 3: Breathe to calm your mind.

- Step 4: With this calmness, open your mind and guide your behaviour to pay attention to the other person's perspective. Be present and listen.

- Step 5: In the moment, ask yourself, "What can I learn from this different perspective?"

- Step 6: After your interaction has finished, ask yourself, "What can I learn from this experience of observing my ego?"

Benefits:

Through this exercise you will be directing your response. You will be taking control of your behaviours instead of reacting to your ego's triggers. You are opening yourself to possibilities and to seeing the complete picture by learning from another's perspective. You are training your mind to be present and not impulsive. You are training yourself to choose your response in any circumstance.

② Target specific manifestations of your ego

For the next ten weeks, once a week choose one manifestation of ego from item #7 of the key summary points of this chapter. Throughout the week, observe your thoughts and behaviours, noticing when your ego manifests itself in this particular way. At the end of each day, take time to journal or reflect upon your findings.

It would be beneficial to ask someone you trust to support you through this process. You can share what you're working on and your challenges, and this person can help point out when your ego manifests itself. It's often easier for others to see your ego's manifestations because they can be more objective. To increase your awareness, it's even better if you can extend your support network to other trusted friends and family. Take their feedback with an open mind and with a grain of salt. Use what resonates with you. Keep yourself accountable for your growth.

Benefits:

During this period, you will be starting to step into your true power. You will be directing your life instead of allowing your ego to direct it. You will be taking ownership of your responses. You will be guiding your mind and uncovering where you have been sabotaging yourself from achieving your highest potential. If you ask others to support you in this process, you will learn even more about yourself, since most of us are limited in our ability to objectively see our own egos at work.

●●●○

PART THREE

GET OUT OF
YOUR MIND

CHAPTER SEVEN

MASTER YOUR EMOTIONS

In the measure that you master yourself, that you control your mental forces instead of being controlled by them, in just such measure will you master affairs and outward circumstances.

—James Allen

Humans are emotional by nature. We have the capacity to experience every shade of our feelings, from love to fear, from joy to sorrow. We have the ability to be aware of our feelings and, through our consciousness, to understand them and give them meaning.

Emotions are a gift if you choose to see them that way. They bring to light where you are in your life, what is essential to you, what you value, and what you don't. Emotions make you take action, and they influence your behaviours, decisions, and mental tranquility. They act as a window to your inner self and offer you opportunities for self-discovery and self-analysis. Your emotions provide you with information about your inner states so you can evolve, learn, and grow. You raise your self-awareness and self-knowledge through your emotions.

I love an analogy used by Dr. Wayne Dyer. It says, "If I were to squeeze an orange as hard as I could, what would come out? Orange juice, of course. Now, let's assume that this orange isn't an orange, but it's you. And out of you comes anger, hatred, bitterness, fear. Why? The answer is because that's what's inside."

Emotions are like a barometer, a key performance indicator that highlights what is going on in your inner world. They manifest themselves when you are having both pleasant and unpleasant experiences.

Unpleasant emotions result when something within you has been triggered, painfully, by external factors. What you are feeling is a defensive reaction that comes from your programming. When you notice these emotions, in that moment of awareness you can bring to light what part or parts of you have been triggered—usually parts that have defined your ego. You bring those catalysts to light through self-examination, using the experiences that generated the emotions. This process will not only help you discover your triggers, but will also support you in giving a new, more positive meaning to your past experiences, uncovering limiting beliefs, reframing your thoughts, and directing your mind to choose how you respond to external factors.

You experience emotions all the time, from subtle to highly charged, and those emotions drive your actions for survival and self-preservation. They are the result of your brain making subconscious decisions based on the perceived reward or the threat from your experience, so you can approach, fight, flee, or stay neutral.

You feel an emotion first, which is immediately followed by an instinctive, often subconscious reaction, and finally a train of thought. If you go back to what you learned about the brain and how it functions, you know that your limbic system, the emotional hub, is one of the first areas to receive information about what you are experiencing externally. It compares this new information with your memories and reacts accordingly, either with fear in case of a threat, or with a reward if it is something pleasurable. After the emotional reaction, you start a train of thought, which with awareness eventually becomes a conscious thought. For instance, you don't consciously choose to think, "This cake is delicious," after your first bite. You first react subconsciously to the taste, feeling the enjoyment of eating it, and then the thought arises, prompting you to have another bite because it makes you feel good.

This process of *emotion* ⇨ *reaction* ⇨ *thought* happens incredibly fast. If you are not sufficiently aware of your thoughts or in tune with your emotions, this process can snowball and affect your equanimity. When an unpleasant emotion is triggered, without your awareness it can rapidly produce negative unconscious thoughts that in turn feed the emotion, which reinforces the train of thought, which continues to feed the pessimistic focus and the unpleasant emotion. This reinforcement of your emotional experience will prolong and escalate the stress reaction in your body, which is working to protect you. It's easy to see how detrimental this process can be to your tranquillity and mental and physical health.

Emotions are neither good nor bad; it's only your thinking that makes them so. They merely provide you with information regarding your programming, which you can use to free yourself from your restless mind and reactionary states.

When you feel happy, you see it as a good thing. When you feel upset, it is a bad thing. But it's important to know that these views are only your *perceptions* because the mind likes to categorize and label everything, giving you necessary information to navigate your world. It is because of those labels that you can recognize a tiger from a kitten. Similarly, your mind classifies and labels intangible things such as behaviours or circumstances, giving them a meaning. The way you are feeling depends on the meaning you give to the circumstances as your mind categorizes them.

You subconsciously create your emotional state from your conditioning and your ego. It is in your nature as a human to do so. You feel a pleasant or unpleasant emotion when external circumstances or people's behaviours match or do not match your subconscious programming or your ego's expectations. If you aren't applying awareness and conscious thinking, you will respond with your automatic programming to any emotion.

For instance, let's say you have a mental list of ways you believe your partner should behave. It's a list you've unconsciously created from your life experiences, and you've been conditioned to think it's correct. If your partner doesn't act in those ways, you may feel upset, react defensively, or want to change or control your partner's behaviour. But if the meaning your programming has ascribed to that behaviour makes you feel happy, you will react in a positive way. The same behaviour from your partner can generate different emotions and reactions based on the beliefs you have and meaning you give to the behaviour.

Now imagine that you are in a meeting, expressing your solution to a problem you and your co-workers are resolving as a team. Suddenly someone challenges your opinion, saying you are wrong and your solution will not work. You may become very upset, thinking, "Who does he think he is? I know this market inside out, and he doesn't get it." Subconsciously, you react, and challenging his expertise, you tell him he is wrong in front of everyone. You are in a defensive mode, ready to defend yourself with a fight-or-flight response. You are driven by your emotion to protect your ego's beliefs. Your mind has taken control over your behaviours without your conscious direction.

Both examples are psychological threats to your integrity. You gave your power away to your subconscious mind, to others, and to circumstances. You allowed it to happen because you were not aware enough to recognize or control your rising emotions. In both examples, notice how your emotions influenced your thoughts, judgment, and actions. The examples show how your emotional state affects the way you think and thus the choices you make.

You may seek to distract yourself from your incessant thoughts and unpleasant emotions. But you cannot run away from yourself; your agitated mind will always return unless you learn how to look within to identify, examine, and master your emotions.

With an open mind, you can learn from your emotions by understanding your reactions. Through studying your reactions, you can unearth the root cause that is disturbing you. Once you're aware of these root causes, the next time you're faced with similar situations you can stop the emotional reactions from controlling you. You may also notice that the unearthed triggers no longer have power over you under those circumstances. You'll see that your emotions are a gift, and the situations you encounter are your teachers.

Through self-awareness and being in harmony with your inner state, you'll find your power—it is within you! Remember, in finding this inner power, you will no longer be bounced around emotionally from life's circumstances and others' behaviours. You will no longer be controlled by your emotional reactions or directed by your subconscious programming. You will have mastered your emotions!

Now let's look at how to understand your emotions.

UNDERSTANDING YOUR EMOTIONS

Many people have been conditioned—through gender, cultural, or personal conditioning—to repress their emotions, mostly the unpleasant ones. They set them aside or bury them instead of welcoming, understanding, and releasing them. This avoidance causes an emotional buildup that takes a toll on their well-being, leaving their bodies operating in constant state of stress. They are living in survival mode. Understanding your emotions will increase your emotional intelligence and foster a centred, objective, and directed mind. Understanding your emotions means undertaking regular self-reflection to help you decipher the messages that your emotions and their triggers are sending you.

Let's do a quick self-awareness exercise and reflection.

Look back at your day for a moment and think about how you felt when you woke up this morning. Were you excited to start your day, or did you have to drag yourself out of bed, feeling unmotivated? How did you feel while having breakfast? What emotions did you experience in your conversations with others or when checking social media or your email? Now, write a quick recap of all the activities you engaged in today before reading this book, and reflect on the emotions they generated and how you reacted to them.

If you conscientiously do this exercise, reflecting on the emotions you experienced up to this moment and your reactions or responses to those emotions, you'll observe that you have a wide range of emotions following you through your daily undertakings.

To understand your emotions more thoroughly, it is important that you identify them and give them a name. For example, when you are feeling stressed, what does it mean? Are you upset, guilty, frustrated, nervous, hesitant, worried, or just busy? If you take a deeper look, you may discover that the stress is a combination of several of those emotions. You may have experienced them at different times, and without examining each one as it occurred, you may be prompted to label them all with the umbrella term *stress*. But when you carefully dissect that stress and identify each specific emotion, you can better examine the cause and triggers.

Once you've named the emotion, welcome it and accept it. Own it! This process of awareness will gradually allow you to get out of your conditioned mind and stop living on autopilot. Remember, unpleasant emotions are rooted in fear, and if you can dig up the trigger, you can begin living fearlessly.

Imagine that you feel guilty for your behaviour in your company's last team meeting, or because of something hurtful you said to your loved one, or because you are hungover—or because of all of those. The guilt you're feeling has your mind repeatedly replaying the situation, which only perpetuates the emotion. Perhaps you are aware of your inner conversation, but you continue the subconscious cycle by not taking control of it. You now can learn, change, heal, and free yourself from the negative emotion.

Now that you're aware of the emotion, breathe, become curious, detach yourself from the situation, and observe it objectively, as if you were watching a movie. Ask yourself some or all of the following questions. The answers will provide you with the information to address and eventually change the emotional trigger. Approach these questions with a wondering mind, seeking to grow from the experience.

- What triggered this emotion?

- Where did this trigger come from?

- What did I immediately tell myself about the situation?

- Where is my interpretation of this situation is coming from?

- What is my reaction telling me about myself?

- What can I learn from this?

- What meaning am I attaching to the situation, both before and after consciously analyzing it?

- Where is this meaning coming from?

- What beliefs do I have that made me react in this way?

- How true are those beliefs to me?

- Where are those beliefs coming from?

- What am I protecting myself from?

- What is it that I am seeking to control?

- Where is my need to control the situation is coming from?

- What do I want to avoid?

- What needs am I seeking to fill that are making me react in this way?

- How can I fill those needs from within myself?

- What can I learn about myself from this situation?

- What can I do differently and more positively next time?

- What is an empowering belief that will support me?

- What empowering meaning can I give to this experience?

- What empowering meaning can I apply to similar past situations?

- What can I do to let go of negative interpretations?

After you ask yourself any of these questions, observe your mind and pay attention to your answers. They will give you information from your subconscious mind. If you were to ask only four questions, the four most important would be:

- What triggered me to feel this emotion?

- Where is this trigger coming from?

- What am I telling myself that is making me feel this emotion?

- Most importantly, what can I learn from this emotion and experience?

Become curious! Through your answers you will discover what you believe about yourself, including:

- Which fears are holding you back

- Where you are placing your worth and value

- Which memories of life experiences are causing you pain

- The situations in which you are a victim of circumstances or people

- The situations in which you are giving away your power

- Why you behave the way you do

- What parts of your ego's image are affected

- What you believe in and value

You will learn more about yourself through this process than you can imagine.

When you do this inner work of questioning yourself, please do it without self-judgment and with a curious mind, compassion, love, and kindness. Through the process you may encounter parts of yourself you don't like or memories that cause you pain, but on the other side of this inner work, you will see the light. Trust that this process will free you from your subconscious programming and the expectations that are causing you pain.

If, after reflecting on your emotions, a part of you still wants to control outside factors, recognize that it is your ego at play. With that awareness, ask yourself:

- Why is important for me to control that person or that situation?

- What is it giving me? Is it safety, a sense of worth, validation?

- If it is any of those, where is that need coming from? What can I do about it?

Through questioning your emotions, you become empowered to choose consciously and direct your mind with purpose. You have the power to reframe the belief, change the story you've been telling yourself, heal the personal experience that caused you pain, and release any negativity. You can create new, productive thoughts, learn from your experiences so you respond differently, and let go of what is not serving you.

It is also an excellent opportunity to achieve more self-knowledge in any situation that produces an emotional reaction, however small or insignificant. For example, when I began working for a multinational company, I noticed I felt a bit anxious while creating my email signature, specifically when I was adding my academic credentials beside my name. I was curious about what aspect of me was apprehensive about it. I soon realized that some part of me believed I was inadequate, and that I should not be proud of my accomplishments—two very limiting beliefs. With awareness comes power, and I chose to take the actions required to move beyond my limiting beliefs, focusing on my strengths and honouring my achievements.

When you find yourself in a situation that is causing your emotions to rise, take these three steps. First, stop and take several big breaths. Second, recognize the emotion and consciously give the situation perspective and, if possible, objectivity. Third, ask yourself the following questions:

- What about this situation is making me feel this way?

- What am I telling myself about this situation?

- Why am I protecting myself, and from what?

- What thought or meaning can I choose right now to support myself?

- What is the most beneficial way to respond to this situation?

- What can I learn about this situation and about myself?

You can treat positive, pleasant emotions in the same way. When you feel happy, engaged, passionate, loving, or are experiencing other feel-good emotions, you can ask yourself:

- What am I doing that is making me feel this way?

- What I am valuing in this situation?

- What beliefs do I have around this?

- What is it about this situation that makes me feel so engaged?

As before, after asking those questions, observe your mind and pay attention to your thoughts as they tell you what is important to you, what you value, and what you love and are passionate about. Begin doing more of it as long as it makes you happy, lights your heart, and helps you connect with the flow of your life.

ACCEPTING YOUR EMOTIONS

It is essential that you accept and honour your emotions.

As we've seen, you—just like most people—have emotions you'd rather not feel because they are painful. The tendency is to reject them, and you will do everything to make that happen, most of the time unconsciously. You'll find ways to distract yourself either by drinking, working, eating, buying things, working out, watching TV, or scrolling through social media—anything that gets you away from feeling your emotion. But distractions are nothing more than that. The emotion is still there—you are just ignoring it, but that won't make it go away.

For instance, I used to feel ashamed, guilty, and embarrassed over a host of different things. I often felt lonely. I would do anything to entertain myself, seeking to escape from my mind and barricade myself from my emotions. My distractions took the shape of drinking, dating, and working. I was working to party and party some more—that was my life. It was causing me to suffer. I remember many times when I wanted to run away, go to another country, and start all over again. I was not happy with myself, my life, or my prospects.

When I accepted my emotions and took the time to understand why I was feeling them, what behaviours they prompted in me, and what I could learn from them, I discovered that I didn't much like myself or the life I was living. I was looking for acceptance. My worth was determined by the opinions of others, my social status, and my material situation. I didn't love myself or have any self-respect. I didn't want to hang out with me. But I didn't want to be alone either.

I was subconsciously sabotaging my life, and that self-awareness was very painful. That new awareness didn't come all at once; it came through the process of peeling back my emotions as they surfaced through circumstances, encounters with other people, and my behaviours and reactions. It was a beautiful and rewarding process of self-discovery, self-awareness, and self-knowledge. I discovered and connected with my true essence and brought inner peace to my life.

You can't run away from yourself; you are always with yourself, and you always will be. You cannot escape from your emotions, your mind, or your ego. Therefore, it is incumbent on you to take care of the relationship you have with yourself. No one else is going to rescue you from yourself.

One of the first steps of my evolution was recognition, acceptance, and understanding of my emotions. This conscious transformation of my life was supported by practising self-compassion while I did this inner work. I focused on myself, on loving me, and on making changes that supported my well-being. I will always be grateful that I found enough wisdom and courage to make that inner journey into conscious living. It is the best work I have ever done, and I will continue doing it for the rest of my life, as there are always new things to learn and new ways to evolve.

Emotions are gifts. They are a window into your self-knowledge. They are opportunities for self-discovery and connecting with your true essence. Every encounter, every circumstance, everyone you meet, anything that triggers you is a teacher and an opportunity to learn.

When you feel unpleasant emotions or when you feel like running away, I invite you to embark on this inner journey and to take the time to reflect on, accept, and honour what you are experiencing so you can release, heal, and evolve. Emotions help you grow and make changes in your life.

In the next chapter, we'll discover how you can unleash the power of your conscious mind.

— KEY SUMMARY POINTS —

(1) Emotions are a gift. In and of themselves, they are neither good nor bad; it is your mind that makes them so. They are a window into your inner world, providing you with information about what is going on within you.

(2) When you are not sufficiently in harmony with your inner self, the snowball effect caused by unpleasant emotions and negative thoughts can have a significant impact on your tranquility and mental health. Thus, mastering your emotions is an essential skill to have in achieving greater well-being.

(3) You feel an unpleasant emotion when an undesired outside experience triggers something within you. These triggers can find their roots in your conditioning, your ego, your expectations, or the meaning you are attaching to your circumstances.

(4) Understanding your unpleasant emotions is an ongoing process of introspection that brings to your awareness those parts of you that were triggered. The unveiling presents you with the opportunity to heal, to move beyond your limitations, and to acquire self-knowledge and inner peace.

(5) It is human nature to want to avoid feeling unpleasant emotions. Are you seeking to distract yourself from them with alcohol, work, food, shopping, TV, etc.? These are only temporary solutions. They hide deeper issues that will continue controlling your life.

(6) You cannot escape from your emotions, your mind, your ego, or yourself.

(7) To develop *emotional mastery*, use these four steps when dealing with unpleasant emotions:

- **First step:** *Recognize* your emotion, and give it a name.

- **Second step:** *Accept* the emotion, don't reject it. It brings you information to help you grow.

- **Third step:** *Understand* your emotion and dissect the information it brings, while being compassionate and kind to yourself.

- **Fourth step:** *Heal* the inner trigger. Give it a new, supportive meaning, create an empowering belief, direct your thoughts, forgive, let it go—and free yourself.

CHAPTER EIGHT

UNLEASH THE POWER
OF YOUR MIND

Every man is what he is because of the dominating
thoughts which he permits to occupy his mind.
—Napoleon Hill

Each thought that you have affects what you do and how you behave. You are always creating, directing, reacting, and experiencing your life through your thoughts.

Your thoughts become your reality. Your thoughts are the instructions and directions you give to your mind, consciously or subconsciously, telling it what to focus on, what to believe in, what actions to take, and what meaning to assign to your circumstances and relationships. Your thoughts also influence your emotions and direct your actions. With conscious effort, you can guide your thoughts to reshape your neural pathways and alter your brain's chemistry. All of it is created by you, but up until now, you've probably been doing it unconsciously.

If you have the power to direct your thoughts, why is it that you are not tapping into it? Why have you been giving your power away to your subconscious mind and your autopilot behaviours?

Your emotions reflect your thought patterns. If your mind has fearful thoughts, you experience worry and anxiety, and if your mind has positive, grateful thoughts, you experience joy and love. Each thought you have influences the attitude you move forward with, and in this way you are creating your destiny. You have the power to choose what kind of thoughts you want to have and what kind you want to nurture. *It is a choice.*

Your thoughts can provide you with information from your subconscious mind. As you now know, the information that feeds the program you use to create your life includes all your beliefs, life experiences, habits, and so on. Observing your thoughts becomes an act of self-discovery and an analysis of your conditioning, and it paves the way for you to consciously start cultivating your mind.

THOUGHT PATTERNS

Remember the mini-mindfulness exercise that you did on page 24? You observed that random thoughts can pop into your mind without your direction. You further noticed that sometimes the thoughts were *not* random—that you were aware, you were present, and you were consciously using your power of choice to direct your thoughts.

Your thoughts, particularly your subconscious ones, come in different patterns, the most common of which begin with a trigger, followed by an instinctive physiological and/or emotional reaction, and then a conscious or subconscious thought about what just happened. The following section will show you some examples of how these patterns can form in your mind and how they can prompt you to react in automatic ways. These examples will help you recognize and become more aware of your own subconscious thought patterns so you can unpack the information they contain.

Trigger ⇨ Emotion ⇨ Thought

Earlier in my career, when I was an estimator in Canada, my manager asked me to call an important client. I was not confident in my business English language skills, and they were the worst over the phone. My conditioned, autopilot response was fear followed by negative thinking.

Trigger: Receiving a request from my manager.

Emotions: Fear and anxiety.

Thought: I can't do it; my English is not good enough.

Reaction: Procrastinating.

Result: Limiting my performance and lowering my self-confidence.

When you find yourself procrastinating, become curious! Ask yourself:

- What am I avoiding?

- What am I telling myself that is reinforcing my fear?

- What are my choices?

- What is the first step I need to take to jump-start my actions?

This approach to examining your reactions and thoughts with curiosity will allow you to unearth your deep-seated beliefs and discover what is holding you back. With awareness, you can take conscious actions and move forward.

Trigger ⇨ Emotion ⇨ Thought

As a sales account manager, I was expected to call senior leaders from my client list, build relationships with them, and connect them with my own company's senior leaders. At first, I was nervous about this task and fearful of not performing well. Those emotions led to thoughts that triggered negative conversations in my mind, ending up in procrastination.

Trigger: Calling the director from XYZ company and organizing a meeting with my director.

Emotions: Fear and nervousness manifesting as hesitance.

Thought: I'll do it after I finish this report.

Thought: You said that last week.

Thought: I know. This time I'll write it on my to-do list.

Reaction: Further procrastinating and giving myself more excuses.

Result: Limiting my career, further lowering my self-confidence, and further entrenching my negative self-image.

When you find yourself in a thought pattern full of excuses, condition yourself to consciously stop this train of thought. With a curious mindset, ask yourself:

- What is holding me back?

- What is it that is preventing me from acting?

- What am I stopping myself from feeling or doing?

- What am I scared of?

With awareness comes transformation, allowing you to gradually overcome your unconscious limitations.

Trigger ⇨ Emotion ⇨ Thought ⇨ Thought ⇨ Emotion

I was travelling to visit some clients outside of Calgary. While I was sitting on the plane waiting to depart, the captain spoke to give us flight information.

Trigger: Hearing a woman's voice.

Immediate emotion: Fear.

Thought: The captain is a woman? Oh no, really?

Conscious thought: What? Why am I thinking like this?

Conscious emotions: Embarrassment, shame.

I remember this thought pattern clearly because it held a powerful message. If I subconsciously was doubting the ability of a woman to be a pilot, it meant that my programmed mind believed that women were not as capable as men of performing their jobs. If that was the case, it meant I also doubted my own capabilities as a woman in my professional life. Again, learn to become conscious of your thoughts. They will bring powerful messages from your subconscious.

Trigger ⇨ Emotion ⇨ Thought

Imagine this scenario happening to you:

Trigger: Forgetting to bring the brochures to the meeting.

Emotion: Frustration.

Thought: Argh! I can't believe I did this. Stupid me!

Reaction: Feeling anger at yourself that escalates into further harmful, negative thoughts.

Result: Negatively affecting your performance in the meeting, eroding your confidence, and more deeply entrenching your autopilot thinking.

Instead of following your ingrained, unconscious patterns of negativity, how could you have used conscious thinking to turn this pattern around? How could you have created a positive outcome for yourself? Perhaps, when you noticed you'd forgotten the brochures, you could have made a creative, conscious choice to think productively: "I forgot the brochures—no big deal. How can I involve my team in creatively solving this?" Perhaps someone from the meeting could pick them up. Perhaps one could be scanned at your office and emailed to the meeting attendees. With an open mind and a positive attitude, you can always find solutions for challenging everyday circumstances.

Trigger ⇨ Emotion ⇨ Thought ⇨ Reaction

Imagine this scenario:

Trigger: Receiving an email from your colleague telling you that he won't have the information you requested on time.

Emotions: Anger and frustration.

Thought: I can't believe it. He's so incompetent! I'm calling his boss.

Reaction: Calling your colleague's boss.

Result: Negatively impacting your mental health and creating conflict.

Notice how the thought "I'm calling his boss" automatically directed your behaviour. It was an impulsive thought, not deliberate or conscious. The thought showed up and you acted upon it. With more awareness, you could have stopped, reflected, and instead asked yourself:

- Where is my anger coming from about this?

- How can I gain control of this situation?

- Which aspects of the situation are in my control and which ones are not?

- What are my choices?

- What is the best way to address this situation, given my options?

- How can I direct my behaviour?

- What can I learn from this?

Can you observe how beneficial it is to stop for a moment, as soon as you feel the emotion? This allows you to reflect on the trigger. With this awareness, you can redirect your thoughts to provide an intentional and productive response to the situation. You will have taken the reins of the situation, preventing the emotion from building up and affecting your judgment.

Thought ⇨ Thought ⇨ Thought

I recall many times when one of my random thoughts led to another associated one, which sparked yet another and then several more until I became conscious of the train of thought and I asked myself, "How did I get there?"

My random trains of thought took many forms similar to this one: "I'm hungry. This meeting is boring. I have so much to do and I'm wasting my time here." These thoughts were quickly followed by: "Dinner at my in-laws last night was delicious. The dog was annoying when it asked for food. Fed my dog under the table when I was a kid. I loved my dog so much, my first pet." My thoughts were associated but not directed; instead, they kept me living in my mind without my awareness. I was missing everything that was happening in the meeting around me.

It is easy enough to see how you are not truly experiencing your life when you're lost in your thoughts rather than being present in the now. Imagine how many opportunities and precious moments you have missed out on just because you've been absorbed in your random trains of thought, allowing your mind to run wild without your conscious direction.

These were some examples of thoughts or inner conversations you might be having in your daily life that are guiding your behaviours, whether emotionally triggered or not. It's interesting to note how, in the examples I provided, I was reacting subconsciously from the combination of trigger, emotions, and thoughts that were directing my life. But I no longer react that way. Nowadays, let's say with the second instance of *trigger ⇨ emotion ⇨ thought* (page 116), I would examine my emotions and ask myself, "What I am feeling hesitant about?" I'd reflect upon it and observe my thoughts. I'd learn that my hesitancy arose because subconsciously I believed that the senior managers at these companies *would not see that I was smart*. I would discover that I was reinforcing self-defeating attitudes about myself such as, "I don't bring any value." Becoming aware of those beliefs allowed me to realize the narrative I was telling myself and how my beliefs were preventing me from seeing my potential.

In the same way that you can uncover your mental programming through your emotional reactions, you can begin bringing awareness to your thoughts and challenge what they are telling you. Question your (formerly) unconscious narrative, asking:

- Where is this thought coming from?

- What is it saying about me?

- How true is this thought to me?

- What belief is it revealing?

- What emotion(s) is this thought generating in me?

- What kind of behaviour is this thought leading me to?

DIRECTING YOUR THOUGHTS

Except for when you're asleep, you are continuously talking to yourself. Now imagine for a moment that the voice in your head has a body of its own, separate from you. This body is like your shadow—it follows you everywhere and constantly tells you what to do, what to believe, what to think. It is also critical of your behaviours and your performance.

Now take a moment and reflect on the following questions:

- Would you enjoy hanging out with this shadow?

- Could it be your best friend?

- Does it show you that it loves you?

- Does it respect you and value you?

- Does it believe in you?

- Does it know your worth?

I asked myself those same questions many years ago, and I came to realize there were aspects of myself that I didn't like. I was my worst critic. I didn't treat myself with love, respect, and care. I was telling myself things I would never tell anyone else I loved. I wasn't valuing myself, so I was looking for external validation to confirm my worth.

So why was I treating myself that way? Because I didn't know how to treat myself any differently.

Many of us have not learned how to be kind, compassionate, and accepting of ourselves. We were not taught how to love ourselves, how to respect ourselves, how to look inward, and how to value the qualities we do possess. Most of us didn't learn to be in tune with our emotions, to be aware of our thoughts, or to be present. Neither were we taught how to examine and understand our inner selves so we can interact consciously with ourselves, others, and the world.

Your conscious or subconscious self-talk will positively or negatively affect your confidence, self-respect, self-worth, and emotional well-being. On the negative side, your inner conversations can cause you to believe that you cannot achieve what you want, go after a goal, be worthy of someone or something, or feel you are good enough. The list goes on. Of course, positive self-talk has the opposite effect—it can lift your spirits, boost your confidence, and help you believe in your ability to accomplish whatever you set out to do in life. In both cases, your thoughts are directing your focus and controlling the direction of your life.

It is so important to look inward and understand your self-talk and thought patterns so you can start discovering who you truly are and the areas in which you are restricting your growth.

Let's look at five areas in your daily life to which you can bring more awareness and focus.

Area 1: When you are your own worst critic

When you begin paying attention to your thoughts, you will become aware of your inner critic. The voice may be judging you harshly, telling you that you cannot do something and why. When you "fail" at something, it criticizes you and makes you feel inadequate. When you recognize these critical thoughts, ask yourself:

- Is this thought part of my conditioning?

- Can I trace it back to when the conditioning began in my life?

- How can I break this conditioning and begin a new, conscious way of directing my thoughts?

- What could my new, conscious thoughts be? (Write them down for future reference.)

Challenge the thought. It's only a thought, after all. Stand up for yourself. Show it the reasons why it is not true.

With the awareness of your negative self-judgment, you can reframe your thought and start talking to yourself as though you were your best friend. After all, if you would not say something negative to someone you love, why would you say it to yourself? I encourage you to talk to yourself with the same respect and love that you would give to others.

The best way to overcome your inner critic is to practise self-compassion by being kind, accepting, and understanding toward yourself. Practising self-compassion also will help you quickly overcome any setback you encounter. Without the hindrance of self-judgment, you will see opportunities to learn and grow.

Area 2: When you fall into victim mode

At certain points in our lives, most of us have victim thoughts and victim behaviours. It's when we are habitually in victim mode that we are jeopardizing our ability to lead a healthy, prosperous, balanced life.

A victim is someone who, with or without awareness, believes they are at the mercy of someone else or something else, and therefore not in control. They blame others and external factors for the situations they find themselves in or for the choices they make. They feel helpless and choiceless because they are giving their power away to others and to outside circumstances.

If you often find yourself in a victim mode, the victim mentality may be benefiting you in some way. Perhaps it provides you with attention from others; their concern about your well-being makes you feel validated and loved. Perhaps it gives you a sense of security because the known feels safer than the unknown. Maybe it is sheltering you from taking responsibility for your life, or maybe you're simply unwilling to endure the discomfort that comes with facing the situation. Being unaware of the benefits you are getting from falling into a victim mentality makes it challenging for you to improve your life circumstances. Unwittingly, you are sabotaging your life.

The best way to identify your victim mentality is by recognizing your internal language and your behaviours. You can notice it when you blame others, complain, or, as said above, experience feelings of helplessness regarding your life and your lack of choices.

One more crucial thing to remember is that you cannot control life's circumstances or people's behaviours, but you *can* control your attitude toward them. A positive, can-do attitude toward challenging circumstances you encounter in your life allows you to free yourself from victimhood and come up with solutions to any obstacles you're faced with.

Here some examples of the thoughts you may subconsciously be creating that are associated with a victim mentality.

"I don't have time."

This means you are a victim of a perceived lack of time. You feel powerless to manage and make decisions around your time. You feel helpless to reach any positive change that you'd like to see in your life because you keep thinking you don't have the time to make the change.

When you hear yourself saying, "I don't have time to do [fill in the blank]," to something you know will benefit your life, examine your thoughts to learn whether this is not just an excuse to stay in your comfort zone. When you notice yourself saying or thinking, "I don't have time," choose to reframe that thought into an ownership statement: "I *have* time; I am *choosing* to do this."

"I can't afford it."

This mindset could mean that you've become a victim of money and of the conditioned importance you give to it. When you tell yourself, "I can't afford it," you remain stuck in your status quo. Subconsciously, you are directing your mind to not seek opportunities or new ideas to obtain the thing you desire or need.

Of course, in certain cases it may be absolutely true that you can't afford something. But often, this thought itself can be disempowering. Close your eyes for a moment and tell yourself, "I can't afford [fill in the blank]." Notice how you feel. You may find that this thinking causes you to feel that you are not in control of your money and you are out of choices. Instead, you can tell yourself, "I choose not to buy this item immediately. Soon, I will find a way to obtain it." Notice how your energy shifts to pull you forward just by directing your thoughts in this way.

Learn to recognize and differentiate between genuine needs or desires and those that have been ingrained in you by parental or societal conditioning, which, if unfulfilled, you may perceive as a lack. You can ask yourself:

- Where is my belief that I need or desire this thing coming from?

- What do I believe buying this thing will give me?

- What needs, psychological or otherwise, do I think having this thing will fill?

- What are my reasons for buying it?

If you have genuine needs or heart-driven desires, you can choose to change your language to words that reflect the possibilities of attaining your goals. With positive language and conscious thought direction, you can empower yourself to take steps to change your financial circumstances and go after the things you truly desire.

Perhaps what you want is simply a conditioned wish and not a genuine desire—for example, you may be feeling down and want to lift your spirits by buying something you don't need. Maybe everyone you know has this item, and you feel as if you're missing out or you're seeking validation from your friends. In those cases, become conscious of the void that acquiring the item would fill. Is it a true lack, or will the void return soon after you've acquired the item? You may find that you don't have to have the item after all, and that the feeling of happiness you'd get from buying it would be fleeting at best.

Start changing your language to show that you are choosing to be in control of your money. Avoid negative words like *not, don't, can't, won't.* Reframe your thoughts in a positive way: "I have other needs right now. I am choosing to save my money. I have enough. I am enough. I'll be able to afford it soon."

"I can't change the world."

The problems in the world can feel overwhelming. How can one person possibly make a difference? Often, you may feel powerless in creating the change you want to see in the world and in taking steps that contribute to something you believe in. This victim thought is preventing you from taking personal responsibility or any actions that could effect changes.

Again, start using positive language that reflects that you are empowered. You can reframe this thought to: "I can change the world with small steps. I am already changing it with every small, positive action that I take."

* * *

Being aware of your victim mindset will help you in making conscious choices. When you recognize a thought that is victimizing you, look at it with a curious mind and ask yourself:

- What am I a victim of?

- What benefit is this giving me?

- What can I do to take responsibility for my life?

- What are my choices and what am I choosing to do?

- What can I control and what can I let go of?

The answers to those questions will help you become aware of your personal conditioning and how and why you are unconsciously choosing to be a victim.

Area 3: When you are ruminating

If you think about the past, you may find yourself ruminating over what you could have done differently. You may feel guilty about your behaviours, causing you to continually overanalyze what happened.

Similarly, rumination can manifest itself when you think about the future. You may feel worried about what will happen, replaying scenarios about what you'll say or how you'll behave, and focusing on what could go wrong.

When you are ruminating, you are trapped in your mind in a negative cycle, thought after thought. And since your mind's tendency is to focus on negativity, it will feed your rumination with similar memories and will imagine worst-case scenarios. This perpetuates the negative cycle until you stop it.

Imagine that you are about to have a meeting with your manager regarding a project you've been working on for some time. You're excited to give her the news about your progress, but just before you leave your office you receive a phone call from one of your suppliers telling you that there's been a three-week delay in production. You know that your manager will be very disappointed. The situation leads you to feel anxiety and frustration. Your mind becomes busy imagining everything that could go wrong, even going as far as to think you could be fired. With all this chaos in your mind, it will be almost impossible for you to have a productive meeting with your manager.

If you find that this kind of catastrophizing is habitual for you, the best way to approach it is by practising mindfulness meditation. When you notice your thoughts are drifting away, refocus on the present moment. Mindfulness can help when you want to reframe any situation, negative or otherwise. You can purposely park the thoughts that caused the rumination and decide to reflect on them later. This will allow you to manage any situation while at the same time training your mind to recognize that you are leading your thoughts and emotions, not the other way around.

Area 4: When you seek validation

Subconsciously, you might be looking to others for validation of your beliefs, opinions, or actions.

You may be seeking validation because of insecurity—you don't want to be rejected or you want to fit in. As you know, your conditioned mind is always trying to protect you from pain, and when it equates rejection with a challenge or threat to your survival, that can mean pain. Your mind will strive to protect you in any way it can, even if it means not being authentic or agreeing to something you find morally reprehensible, just to please others.

For example, I recall looking for validation of my worth through dating. I would say anything I believed the person I liked wanted to hear so he would like me back. I was not being authentic; I was seeking to be what I thought the other person wanted me to be rather than being myself.

When you look for acceptance and approval from others, you diminish your value, your self-worth, and your confidence. You don't trust yourself, you don't love yourself, and you believe your worth is based in the opinions of others.

Bringing awareness to your mind when you are seeking validation is the most essential step in learning to find validation within yourself and not from others. Ask yourself the following questions:

- Where is my need to have others validate or confirm my opinions, beliefs, or actions coming from?

- Why am I insecure about expressing my truth? Where is this insecurity coming from?

- What do I gain when I am validated?

- Why can I not trust myself? Where is this uncertainty coming from?

These questions will help you understand where the need for validation comes from. Maybe life experiences conditioned you to seek validation for protection, or perhaps it is your ego at play. Whatever the cause is, you will be at the mercy of your unconscious behaviours until you understand where this need for validation is coming from and you learn to fulfill the need yourself.

Area 5: When you use conditioned language that lacks possibilities

The language you use in your daily life may be unwittingly conditioning you, to the point where you're not even aware you're using it. Your choice of words consciously or subconsciously creates emotions that direct your behaviours and creates limitations in your mind. Your language governs your actions.

The word *try* is a great example. You use it often when you want to communicate that you will attempt to do something or that you will put an effort into it. Have you ever thought of what saying *try* implies? When you use this word, you are implying there's still a chance you will *not* do it or *not* give your best; you are telling your mind that is not necessary to complete the task. You leave yourself an escape route and open yourself to excuses, limiting yourself right out of the gate.

Let's say you tell yourself, "I'll try to start meditating tomorrow." You are implying there's a possibility that you won't meditate. Instead, if you say, "I'll start meditating tomorrow morning," you are telling your mind that you *will* meditate in the morning, leaving no room for excuses. Either way, the words you use in your communication with yourself and with others determine your behaviour and guide your energy.

I invite you to do a quick exercise in order to feel the difference when you remove *try* from your dialogue.

After you finish reading these instructions, close your eyes, take five full, big breaths, and think about something you want to do. In your mind or aloud, say, "I will try to start [fill in the blank]." Pause, and feel the energy and emotions you are experiencing.

Next, take three full, big breaths and in your mind or aloud, say, "I will start [fill in the blank]." Pause, and feel the energy and emotions you are experiencing.

After people do this exercise, most feel uncommitted when they say the first sentence—it lacks energy. With the second sentence, they feel more confident and committed—it has an energy that incites them to move forward.

To recap, there are two critical things to be aware of in this exercise. The first is that the words you use guide your behaviour. The second is that the power words have and how you use them create emotions that either inhibit you or encourage you to move forward.

Another widely used word is *hope*. In general, it speaks of an optimistic attitude that helps you move forward. But the word also carries a different meaning that could be hindering you, depending on the usage and the context.

Let's imagine that you say to your colleague, "I hope my presentation goes well." This implies the possibility that it will *not* go well. Subconsciously, you are not directing your energy to showing up for your presentation with your very best attitude and confidence. If you say instead, "I *know* my presentation will be great," you create the positive emotion and energy required to support you moving forward. You create an inner attitude that will help you be more confident and assertive in your presentation.

There are other such ambiguous words that society has conditioned us to use. We often use them without the awareness of the impact they can have on our energy and behaviour. Here are some examples.

From "I should" to "I choose to"

When you use the word *should*, you are implying that you have an obligation to do something. It also suggests that you don't have the willpower to decide whether you will do it, or that you are burdened with expectations and responsibilities (from yourself, your work, family, friends, or society) that you don't necessarily want to fulfill. Using *should* excuses you from the responsibility of making your own choices, and can drag you down and sap your motivation.

When you use the word *choose*, it means you are the one who is deciding; you are stepping into your power of choice. When you choose to do an activity, you feel more in control, more motivated, eager, and engaged to act. Your use of the word *choose* will energize and fortify your decisions.

If you use *should* to indicate an obligation rather than a desire, ask yourself:

- Why do I believe this is an obligation for me? Where is this belief coming from?

- Why do I feel such indecision?

- What beliefs do I have that are preventing me from making my own choice to do it?

- What excuses am I giving myself?

From "I have to" to "I choose to"

Comparable to *should*, when you say, "I have to" or "I must," the implication is that you have a strict obligation to do the thing in question. This usage suggests that you are telling yourself you don't have any control or any other alternatives. As a result, your brain will not look for any, and you'll feel unmotivated to take action. The truth, though, is that you always have other options. However, those alternatives may be even less palatable to you, so your subconscious mind convinces you that you have only one option.

When you are aware that you have more than one option, you can select the one you believe best fits your circumstances. Just the fact that you are telling yourself, "I choose to," means you're teaching your mind that you are in control, and that helps you move forward.

Finally, you can always ask your mind to look for alternatives. What other options are available to you? As you allow the answers to come, you are opening yourself to new possibilities.

If you still feel that you "have to" do something, ask yourself:

- Why do I fear this situation?

- What am I avoiding?

- What can I control about the situation and what can I let go of that's not in my control?

From "I have a problem" to "I have an opportunity"

When you think or say, "I have a problem," you are putting yourself in a defensive mode. You are focusing on the threat only, which is not allowing you to see other alternatives. Psychologists and others have suggested many ways to reframe a problem, including deciding there are no problems, only solutions; that it's not a problem, it's a challenge; that the glass is half full, not half empty; that for every problem, there is a solution; that the human capacity for new ideas is infinite, and so on.

Personally, I choose to say, "I have an opportunity," and then become curious about the possibilities. *Opportunity* and *possibility* are positive, exciting words; they direct the mind away from the threat and the worrisome feeling. This conscious directive will support you in embracing previously unknown possibilities. Solutions come with a calm and curious mind, not with a chaotic, uneasy one. By being open to solutions, you become more creative, and you learn from each experience.

When you encounter a challenging situation that you label as "a problem," change your language. Become curious, and ask yourself:

- How can this be an opportunity for me?

- What can I learn from this situation?

- What are my options?

- How can I see this situation from a different perspective?

* * *

We've discussed some examples of unconstructive language you may have been conditioned to use by your own fears and by society. It is essential that you be alert and conscious of when you are using this conditioned language. Whether you are having conversations with yourself or with others, start using words that suggest possibilities, opportunities, resources, and abundance. Select language that supports choices and that doesn't leave you at the mercy of circumstances. Choose language that states that you are in control, that you are in power.

When you become more conscious of the language you use in your thoughts and speech, you'll begin to realize the effect it has in your life. In these moments of awareness, you can unlock your mind and your ability to direct your thoughts and guide your mind to stillness and emotional well-being.

Until now, you may never have questioned what your mind was telling you. Now it's time for you to listen to your inner self and change the script.

— KEY SUMMARY POINTS —

(1) Your thoughts become your reality. You create, direct, and experience your life with the direction of your thoughts.

(2) Every thought has an effect and informs how you perceive your life.

(3) The emotions you experience are the result of your self-created way of thinking. If you have fearful thoughts, you experience fear. If you have loving thoughts, you experience love. You choose which thoughts you have and which thoughts you feed.

(4) You can unleash the power of your mind when you direct your thoughts, which helps you stop them from running wild and directing your life.

(5) By observing and being aware of your thoughts, you develop the ability to understand their nature. With this understanding, you can uncover your programming, discover your ego triggers, and recognize the meaning you give your circumstances.

(6) Your self-communication can impact your life positively or negatively.

(7) When you become your own worst critic, when you victimize yourself, when you ruminate, and when you use language that lacks possibilities, start directing your thoughts more positively and guiding your self-conversations.

CHAPTER NINE

REMOVE THE FOUR MOST COMMON LIMITING BELIEFS

What lies behind us and what lies before us are tiny matters compared to what lies within us.
—Ralph Waldo Emerson

Each of us has unique, deep-rooted beliefs that are, in some ways, limiting us. I trust that by now, you are already working on how to identify yours—by paying attention to your thoughts and emotions when they are triggered. Some limiting beliefs are common among many of us. I have found four predominant ones in my personal experience and in working with my clients.

In this chapter, I will discuss these four limiting beliefs at length. Perhaps, as you read, you'll discover that you already know of some of them. If you do, you can skip to the next chapter—or continue reading and give yourself the opportunity to hear a different perspective. You can reinforce your own ideas about these beliefs and acquire more tools to remove their influence and their limitations. Let's get into them now.

I AM NOT GOOD ENOUGH

This "I am not good enough" belief may sound very familiar to you. It is probably the one belief that resonates with almost all of us. Women, in particular, may fall victim to this kind of belief and also may be more aware of it. Men may also have this deep-rooted belief, but often it is buried beneath the conditioned way they perceive themselves and their masculinity.

This belief stems from different roots. Often it comes from a conditioned model of self-perfection your mind has created—an unattainable model. It may have arisen from your upbringing, when you sought love and validation and didn't always get it, or from the feeling that you don't measure up to others. It may stem from a need to avoid the emotional pain that might come with failure, embarrassment, shame, or rejection. It can manifest as a lack of self-confidence, self-esteem, and self-acceptance.

Fundamentally, this belief is based in fear. This fear drives you to fill a perceived empty space within you and to strive to become your self-created flawless model. Notice that I use the word *perceived* because it is only a perception: you believe in it based on your past experiences and conditioning.

This belief prompts your mind to create a narrative. For example, perhaps you are telling yourself:

- I don't have enough experience to apply for that job.

- I'm not smart enough to apply for that job.

- I'm not smart enough to give my opinion.

- I'm not important enough for my opinion to matter.

- She is more confident than I am.

- I'm not at their level.

- I don't have what it takes to [fill in the blank].

- I am not good enough for [fill in the blank] or to be [fill in the blank].

- I am not attractive enough.

- I am not strong enough.

You can see how the list could go on for pages as you add almost any quality into the sentence, "I am not [fill in the blank] enough." But you *are* enough, just as you are, and it is your choice to overcome this "I am not good enough" belief.

To break away from it, when you recognize the negative voice in your mind telling you that you're not good enough for something or someone, stop, ask yourself the following questions, and reflect on your answers:

- In what way do I think that I am not enough?

- Where is this belief coming from?

- Is it mine? Did I create it through my life experience? Or is it someone else's and I am following it just to conform?

- What are five exceptions to this belief?

- Where is my need to compare myself to others coming from?

- What are the "measuring" standards I am using? Where are they coming from?

- To whom am I trying to prove myself?

- Where is my need for perfectionism coming from?

- How true is this belief to those people who love me?

- What can I do to accept and appreciate myself as I am?

- What am I valuing in this?

- What can I value about myself in this?

- What actions can I take to feel and know that I am already enough for [fill in the blank]?

Next, strongly invalidate the voice in your mind. To do this, imagine the voice is another person. Thank the voice for trying to protect you, and with compassion, give the voice different reasons why you are more than good enough. Each time you hear the voice, direct your mind by thinking about moments in your life when you successfully overcame a similar situation and how you made it happen. You can further direct your mind to focus on your strengths and the learning opportunities available in this current situation to help you grow. Soon, you'll come to recognize that the negative voice was all in your head, you subconsciously created it, and thus you can overcome it.

Become curious about what your mind is telling you and change the script to a supportive one. Awareness and reflection are the key to transcending this false belief.

I AM NOT WORTH IT

The second limiting belief I've found to be prevalent is "I am not worth it." Self-worth is the value you give to yourself; it also encompasses self-love. It's possible or even probable that no one has taught you how to love yourself, see your value, or appreciate your worth. Very likely, you were conditioned to see worthiness and accept it in others but not in yourself.

Much like "I am not good enough," this belief has you convinced that others are better than you. As result, you are constantly comparing yourself to them and to what they own, their accomplishments, their financial resources, their partner, their behaviours, their position at work, their looks, their degrees, and so on.

This belief can also have you feeling that you don't deserve something or that you are worthy only when you:

- Accomplish a certain goal

- Have certain qualities or own specific things

- Become a particular type of person

- Associate with certain people

Subconsciously, you may be sabotaging your life by believing you are not worthy.

If you hold this belief, in the same way your ego manifests itself, you will need validation from others through praise of your behaviours, your material goods, your social status, your career status, your appearance, or your achievements, among other things. In your need for validation, you also long for love and acceptance. If you fail to receive praise, love, or acceptance, you may automatically and subconsciously feel unworthy. But waiting for others' approval and love is a futile endeavour—it means you are giving away the power over your self-worth to others. Ultimately, you can't measure your value by anyone's standards except your own. Nurturing self-worth starts with inner work that allows you to connect with yourself and develop ways to respect, value, accept, and love yourself. If you do this self-examination, you'll discover that your self-worth doesn't need to rely on external validation; nor is it based on your life experiences. Self-worth comes from within, and only you can determine it.

It will help if you recognize that this belief may have been passed on to you by your family, social circle, and society. Or it may have been unconsciously created by your personal experiences. You may have been conditioned to believe that others are more worthy than you because they have more of [fill in the blank], or that others are less worthy than you because they have less of [fill in the blank]. Or perhaps you believe you are not worthy because you did something you feel ashamed of. Or maybe it's simply that you are not accepting yourself fully and completely.

To overcome this belief, start by recognizing times when you are seeking validation or comparing yourself to others using such judgments as "They are better than me," and "I am better than them," or when you catch your inner voice telling you that you are not valuable. Another way to bring awareness to times when you feel unworthy is by observing yourself. Explore the areas of your life in which you're lacking self-acceptance or self-respect or allowing others to disrespect you. Check whether you are not treating yourself with the same regard you show others.

When you find any of the above situations, ask yourself:

- Why do I believe I am not worthy? Where is this belief coming from?

- Where is the need to compare myself with others coming from? What is it giving me?

- Where is the belief that others are better than me coming from?

- What is making me feel unworthy?

- What about this particular situation is making me feel unworthy?

- Where is my need to seek validation coming from? What is it giving me?

- In what ways am I not respecting and valuing myself?

- Where is the belief that I am not valuable coming from?

- What void am I seeking to fill?

- What needs am I seeking to fill? How can I nurture them?

- How can I love and appreciate myself more?

Finally, become the most compassionate person possible toward yourself. Practise self-compassion by talking to yourself as though you were talking to the person you love most in the world. Accept yourself unconditionally, honour your past experiences, and nurture your self-love. Through reflection, you can examine painful life experiences that formed this belief. Once you become aware of the cause or causes, direct your mind, telling yourself the same things you would say to someone you love when they are feeling unworthy. Change the narrative in your subconscious.

Choose *you!* Begin making changes that honour the magnificent self that you already are, and start believing that you are entirely worthy, accepted, and loved.

I CAN'T DO IT

Why do we so often sabotage ourselves by telling ourselves we can't do something—before we even go for it? As we've discussed, it is our subconscious at work trying to protect us.

Have you noticed that sometimes you want to do something with all your heart, but your mind starts feeding you all kinds of excuses for why you shouldn't do it? It tells you what will go wrong and why you will fail. Perhaps you are fully aware while telling yourself that you can't do something, but you might not be conscious of the underlying negative narrative.

The "I can't do it" belief is often based on a fear of failure or how other people might judge you. When your self-talk repeatedly tells you, "I can't do it," it becomes reinforced in your subconscious, which holds you back and prevents you from accomplishing what you are seeking to do. Regardless of whether you are conscious of what you're telling yourself, your mind knows it and will be looking to the outside world for validation that indeed you can't do it. Your mind creates excuses to stick to your conditioned pattern, keeping you trapped. Now that you know this, when you think, "I can't do it," look at the facts, understand your situation, and reflect on how accurate your belief is for your circumstances. Ask yourself:

- Am I giving myself excuses to get out of the thing I want to do?

- If so, what are they?

- What belief have I created that prompts me to think I can't do this?

- Where is that belief coming from?

- Is the belief mine or was it imposed by the external world?

Furthermore, think about situations in your life when you accomplished something that at first you thought was unachievable, and then reflect on what traits, what strengths, and what mindset allowed you to succeed.

Do your best to *not* choose in fear; instead, open your mind to let fear out of your life.

I DON'T HAVE A CHOICE

This is a common belief that people fall back on, often without being aware of it. As it suggests, this belief prompts you to think that you are out of choices and that you are stuck in your situation permanently.

Let's take the example of one of my clients. Entrenched in a leadership position, he felt he had no other option but to stay in his job because so many people depended on him, and his team was not ready for his departure. The feeling of being stuck, and the associated guilt, would not allow him to see all his options. The simple fact that he remained in his position implied that he had already chosen the only option he thought was available to him, while subconsciously rejecting all other options. This belief made him feel powerless and like a helpless victim of the situation.

When you think, "I don't have a choice," you are directing your mind to believe there are no choices. As a result, that will be precisely what you experience, and you'll feel trapped.

To overcome this belief, consciously start looking for alternatives, even when you feel you don't have any. The fact is that plenty of options exist for you. You are under the impression that you don't have choices only because your fear limits you to one option to protect you from the pain that choosing another might bring. Ask yourself: What are two other alternatives for me? If nothing comes up, stay with the question, and trust that the answer will come to you. Just opening your mind to the possibility of other options will in itself open up new possibilities. Knowing you have choices even if you are not yet aware of them is empowering and liberating.

Here is an example of how options present themselves when we are open to them. I was helping a client restructure one of the departments in his company. At that time, he was aware that changes were required in the structure of his company to improve performance and productivity, yet he felt stuck, trapped in old patterns and conditioned ways of doing things. I guided him to think outside the box and to consider that more options are always available. I asked him the simple question, "What are your options?" He listed the ones he had in mind but was hesitating over, and I continued asking, "What is another option?" until we exhausted all apparent possibilities. This exercise eventually sparked an idea for a final option that neither of us had thought of at first. When you open yourself to considering new alternatives, you begin actually seeing them—it's that straightforward.

In this brief chapter, we looked at how to recognize the most common conditioned beliefs, you reinforced some concepts if you already knew them, and you acquired further tools to help get yourself out of your own way. In the next chapter, we will examine your power of choice.

— KEY SUMMARY POINTS —

(1) "I am not good enough" is probably the most common belief, the one that affects most people. It has multiple roots that stem from your conditioning, and it causes you to think others are better than you, that you aren't measuring up in various ways. This belief can easily become a liability by interfering with your ability to take action and by making you feel that you already don't have what it takes.

(2) The "I am not worth it" belief causes you to compare yourself to others, seeking validation and yet never feeling that you measure up. The root of this belief is lack of self-acceptance and self-love.

(3) The "I can't do it" belief is based on the simple fear of failure and judgment. Look at the facts and see how true it is for you, and be aware that this belief is largely a product of your conditioned mind.

(4) You always have a choice, but the "I don't have a choice" belief makes you think otherwise. Open yourself to the unlimited possibilities that surround you.

CHAPTER TEN

YOUR POWER OF CHOICE

Choice implies consciousness—a high degree of
consciousness. Without it, you have no choice.
Choice begins the moment you disidentify from
the mind and its conditioned patterns,
the moment you become present.
—Eckhart Tolle

The power of choice means using your free will to decide how to direct your life. Choice is a gift that you have as a human being. But it is not always used wisely or consciously.

Take a few minutes to think about the decisions you have made today, as many as you can remember from the moment you awoke to this point in your day. Write them down if you like. Did you wake up and jump out of bed or set the alarm to snooze for ten more minutes? What did you choose for breakfast? What did you choose to wear? Everything you did was a choice, including picking up this book to read. Take a couple of breaths and reflect on your choices.

If you do this reflection, you will notice that you are making decisions every single moment about everything you do. The consequences of your decisions are continually shaping your life. How you experience your life is a reflection of each decision you make along the way.

Most people are aware of the big decisions they make, such as purchasing a car, going on vacation, or asking someone to marry them. Those are decisions that require a great deal of consideration. But how aware are you of the daily, minute-by-minute choices you make? And from what frame of mind are you making them?

Most of your choices, from small daily decisions to substantial ones, come from your conditioned mind and your ego. Did you select that programming? Did you choose your beliefs and ideas about the world? Now that you have read most of this book, you most likely can guess that the answer is no. You didn't choose them; they were passed on to you and you absorbed them.

In the last three chapters, you learned about the power of your emotions to help you expose your conditioning and your ego. You learned about bringing awareness to your thoughts and tapping into the power of your mind to direct your thoughts, your behaviours, and your self-communication. You learned about your conditioned beliefs. As a result, you can now probably appreciate that awareness is the first step to a conscious transformation. With awareness you discipline yourself to consciously choose how to respond to any situation, see possibilities in every circumstance, and purposely direct your mind. In the rest of this section, we'll look at the areas of your life where you have the opportunity to use your power of choice and start living and deciding consciously.

CHOOSE YOUR THOUGHTS AND WORDS

Having done the simple exercises in this book, you now know that you have the ability to observe your mind and your thoughts. You also have the ability to choose the thoughts and words you use to express yourself in any given situation.

When you consciously observe your thoughts, you learn to understand them, to know where they come from, and to select those that motivate you, offer possibilities, and benefit your well-being rather than those your mind randomly feeds you.

You've already practised choosing your thoughts in the mindfulness exercise on page 24, so you know how to do it. It is now your decision to observe your mind and select your thoughts as often as possible, especially when you are feeling agitated.

CHOOSE THE MEANING OF YOUR CIRCUMSTANCES

Nothing in life is entirely good or bad, or entirely right or wrong. It is your thinking and definitions that make it so.

As you go about your life, people and circumstances come and go, both pleasant and unpleasant, but they are that way because you perceive them that way. You put them inside a box with a label designating the meaning you have assigned them. The suffering you experience from unpleasant circumstances is a consequence of that assigned meaning. Pain and suffering are not the same thing. You may feel pain—in some cases, it is inevitable—but suffering is optional. You can choose to observe and accept pain without suffering and dwelling on it.

Life is always evolving. Change is part of the flow of life—even the air you take in is different with every breath. But because you are a human being, the tendency of your mind and your ego is to control that flow. Thus, you resist the change when events in your life don't match your expectations. It is then that you suffer. The opposite occurs when your circumstances match your expectations—you feel joyful and you welcome the events.

When you accept an unpleasant life circumstance and see it as it is, you are empowered. When you see it without labels as simply something that happened to you, you can work with it. With this approach, you are not making things worse by allowing your mind to ruminate only on the negative. You cannot change what happened to you, but you can decide how you want to respond and the meaning you wish to give to the situation. There is so much power in acceptance. Acceptance will help you ease and release the resistance and suffering you experience when you attempt to control circumstances. I encourage you to accept them, to release the resistance. To support yourself, you can ask:

- What am I here to learn?

- From what other perspective can I see this situation?

- How can I see it as an opportunity for me?

- How can I grow and evolve from it?

Yes, some situations in life are more painful than others, and some can cause you deep sorrow or overwhelming fear. At the same time, the consciousness within you has the capacity to see them as part of life. Once you accept this, you have the power to decide how to approach the situation and the meaning you give it. I am not saying it is easy or simple, but it is certainly possible.

Perhaps some painful events in your life are still causing you distress. They may have shaped who you are, but you still have the authority to reassign a new meaning to them. You can choose to see the situation from a different perspective, accept it, and forgive. It doesn't mean you are validating what occurred, but you are giving it a new, supportive meaning. You are taking your power back; the situation no longer has to define you or control your life.

Approach new and old circumstances in your life with a mindset of openness, acceptance, and understanding while treating yourself with kindness and compassion. If you are aligned with a certain faith, you know that anything that happens in life has a higher purpose. If not, if you can't see the purpose at the moment, trust that one day you will look back and connect the dots to see your experience clearly.

A good place to start developing this mindset is through small situations over which you have no control. For example, the weather. Imagine that for months you have planned a romantic getaway to the beach, and precisely on the weekend you've chosen, the forecast calls for cold and windy weather. Since you have been conditioned to think "nice weather" means sunny and warm, you'll feel upset and disappointed with anything else. But you can choose a new label for it. You can think that instead of a lousy day, it is a beautiful misty morning with some clouds and rain, and you are holding hands and laughing with your lover on the beach.

Choose your perceptions to get the most out of your life.

CHOOSE TO BE GRATEFUL

Choosing to cultivate gratitude in our lives is a beautiful gift we can give to ourselves. Often, we take for granted the gifts we receive every day, and the pleasures of giving in return.

Become aware of the things you are grateful for in your life. Have them present daily, and honour them. When you are grateful, you boost your energy, which helps you cope with stress and setbacks. When you are grateful, you feel good about yourself and the abundance in your life. This state of gratitude helps you see different perspectives, and it supports positive behaviours and choices.

Gratitude will also help improve your relationship with others, your health, and your engagement in anything you do, because you won't take these things for granted. You'll value and appreciate them and give them the respect and love they deserve.

Furthermore, by choosing to be grateful, you'll train your

mind to focus on the good things in your life, so it gradually stops defaulting back to its negative tendencies. Gratitude becomes a cycle that begins with a conscious choice and leads to a new habit, which leads to the enhancement of your life.

You can start the day by setting an intention to be aware of one thing for which you are grateful. During your day, recognize it, appreciate it, and honour it—as often as possible. Then, before you go to bed, bring into your awareness three more things for which you are grateful, and journal about them or simply write them down.

Additionally, you can include your family, friends, and colleagues by asking them what they feel grateful for. By making a habit of asking one another what you are grateful for, together you can enrich your lives.

CHOOSE A CURIOUS MINDSET

Up until now, you have probably defined almost every situation in your life using the same programmed framework, and your mind has become conditioned to prompt you to maintain the status quo.

In your life you will encounter people who challenge your opinions, and you'll also encounter undesirable circumstances when things don't go your way. For instance, imagine you are in a meeting or having a discussion with some friends, sharing your opinion, when someone voices an opposing point of view. Your ego is offended, and it reacts by defending your perspective. You want to win the argument to prove you are right.

This duality of right or wrong, win or lose is a psychological defence mechanism that creates separation between people by not recognizing or accepting other people's perspectives. It prevents you from connecting with others and from developing meaningful relationships. In a corporate setting, it prevents you from collaborating in a team effort, or even from advancing in your career. The separation caused by this duality prevents you from seeing and attaining benefits for the group since your focus is on yourself.

A loftier way to approach any of those situations is to choose a learner mindset, to cultivate a curious mind. You will begin to recognize that any encounter can be a gift that allows you to grow. With a curious mind, ask yourself, "What can I learn from this situation?" Pay attention to any emotional resistance the situation creates. Ask yourself, "What definition am I giving to the situation that's making me feel this way?"

To open your mind and get out of the box created by your conditioned, limited perspective, it's essential to develop curiosity and to approach any circumstance with the mindset of a student who is eager to learn from life. A curious mindset that is ready to learn helps you approach life with more ease and peace because you're less rigid in your way of thinking and your expectations. You will move toward growth and evolution, wisdom and mastery, and begin seeing possibilities you hadn't imagined.

There's no better time to start developing a curious mindset than when you feel you need to be right and others wrong. If, say, your friend is offering an opinion you disagree with, pay attention to the rising of your emotions, and when you are in this awareness, pause and choose to not react. Then ask yourself:

- What can I learn from this moment and this situation?

- How can I be more open to and understanding of my friend's opinions?

Continue with an open mind to listen to the person's perspective. When you choose to approach the conversation with a curious mind, you'll start seeing the situation from different angles. Because you are learning from another perspective, your knowledge and empathy will expand.

It's key to remember that you don't necessarily have to agree with the other person. Instead, respectfully ask why they feel the way they do; you are very likely to learn something new and to strengthen that relationship.

Later in your day, to achieve even greater self-awareness, reflect on the situation by asking yourself:

- What was I protecting myself from?

- If I crave others' approval so much, where does that need for validation come from?

- Similarly, why is it so important for me to prove my point? What is it giving me?

- Why can't I acknowledge that they might actually be right?

- How can I nurture the part of me that has this need rather than seeking validation from others to fill it?

Having a curious mindset contributes to your evolution and well-being. Open your mind and recognize that your life journey is not about being right or wrong, winning or losing, or getting what your conditioned mind wants. It is about your growth, evolution, and contribution. That is freedom, that is truly living, and it all starts with a conscious choice to work on your inner self.

CHOOSE YOUR FOCUS

Every single moment of your day, you are choosing what to focus on. It is happening whether you are conscious of it or not. Your focus may already be challenged by a non-directed mind that is engaged with random trains of thought. Furthermore, your attention is spammed by external stimuli such as emails, texts, phone calls, people, social media, etc., distracting you from the task at hand. It is important to train your mind to not only select a focus but also to avoid distractions, rather than allowing your programming or external factors to rob you of your attention. You can train and discipline your mind by consciously directing your impulses.

For example, if you notice you have the impulse to check your phone, stop and choose to do otherwise. You can practise focusing in countless other situations, such as when you have a craving for sweets or when you want to pass a slow driver on the highway. You will be delaying gratification and training your mind to know that you are in the driver's seat.

CHOOSE TO BE PRESENT

Your life is happening right now! By choosing to live in the present moment, you will be waking up to your life. Direct your awareness to experience it.

Being in the present moment helps you achieve inner peace and equanimity. It is a state available to you that may have been overshadowed by the busyness of your mind, a lack of consciousness, and our societal obsession with multi-tasking.

By being present, you will rejoice in the company of your family, your friends, and in all those special moments that make life a treasure. You will increase your productivity and performance, improve your relationships, and connect with yourself at a deeper level. When you are present, you direct your thoughts, emotions, and behaviours. The result is improved mental, emotional, and physical health—in other words, you improve your overall well-being.

An excellent way to achieve presence and inner peace is by meditating. Meditation is a practice, like working out, that becomes easier the more you do it. Meditation helps you train your mind to be still, focused, and centred. In this stillness you can hear your heart and clear your mind of distracting thoughts.

You can look at meditation as a concentration exercise that allows you to observe your mind, discover how it is getting in your way, and bring it back into focus. There are plenty of techniques for practising meditation. You start by placing your full attention on a thought or an object of your choice such as your breathing, your body, a mantra, a sound, or an image.

Mindfulness, as a meditation technique, helps you focus your mind to be in the present experience. You can practise it anywhere, simply by choosing to focus on the task at hand and being immersed fully in the moment. You can practise it as part of your daily activities, such as when you are eating (focus on savouring the food), or when you are waiting for someone (focus on feeling your breath), or when you are exercising (focus on experiencing your body). Direct your mind to focus on all your senses in everything you do.

Meditation requires practice, discipline, and patience. Initially, your mind will go to great lengths to avoid such hard work. When you notice that happening, when your mind is telling you to give up or when you feel uncomfortable, that is the very moment for you to direct your mind, without judgment, back to its focus. You don't allow your mind to dictate your focus. Train your mind to achieve stillness and follow your direction without resistance.

By using meditation to direct your mind, you are also practising self-control, because it is only when you are guiding your thoughts that you can control your actions.

CHOOSE YOUR RESPONSES

You have the power to manage your responses rather that have them dictated by your mind's autopilot reactions. Since your conditioned, autopilot reactions are faster than your thought process, a key part of your training is to slow your reactions and consciously think before they take over.

Again, you can accomplish this through meditation. With the practice of meditation, you become increasingly in tune with your inner self. When you are triggered, you will come to recognize the emotion as soon as it arises, and you can then consciously direct your thoughts and your response.

Research shows that meditation shrinks the amygdala, thus slowing its reaction. As you learned in Chapter 4, the amygdala is responsible for the fight-or-flight response. Also, meditation thickens the prefrontal cortex, the rational part of your brain, which helps you to be thoughtful in your responses. The combination of both will help you choose your response, overriding your brain's protection mechanism.

Another way to manage your responses is through a process of introspection. By examining and learning to understand your past triggers, emotions, and reactions, you can gain self-knowledge so you respond and react differently in future. Through this self-awareness process, you will learn to be prepared when something similar happens.

CHOOSE TO TAKE RESPONSIBILITY FOR YOUR LIFE

It's very simple—if you are a healthy, able-bodied adult, only you can take responsibility for your life. No one else can live it for you. You are the person experiencing your life, the only one who knows your thoughts, your emotions, your intentions. Only you can bring awareness to your thoughts instead of letting them run wild, without a direction. No one else can do certain things for you—no one can eat healthily, go to the gym, or meditate for you. No one can learn for you or do the work of introspection. These are personal choices; they are your responsibility. It is your life!

If you look around, you may realize that you have grown up in a culture of blame. People often blame others for what is happening in their lives. They find excuses for not doing what is necessary to be fulfilled and happy. For instance, most people do not take responsibility for their emotional state.

Let me elaborate. Imagine that one day you say to a friend, "This person [fill in the name] makes me so angry." Think about that for a moment. It sounds as if anger was *forced* on you. In reality, this person did not make you do or feel anything. Anger was a product of your mind, of your own creation. You created it through your thoughts and the meaning you gave to the situation. The person's behaviours triggered something within you that irritated you. But instead of blaming them for your anger, it is your responsibility to understand its root causes. In becoming aware of your emotional reactions, you'll see why blaming others, being defensive, or playing the victim is pointless; worse, it is detrimental to your well-being.

You'll find it empowering when you choose to take responsibility for your past decisions, even if some of them have landed you in a bad situation. Often, the tendency is to blame others or yourself by ruminating on what you could have done differently. When you find yourself doing that, be compassionate and kind to yourself above all. Know that you made certain choices based on the information and resources available to you at the time. Then, with your new knowledge, adopt a curious mindset and explore what you can learn from those past decisions.

I encourage you to become aware of times when you may be subconsciously asking others to make decisions for you. Perhaps you fear having to face consequences for a decision that will force you to deal with the unknown and cause you emotional distress. Your indecision may manifest itself in your career, in your family, or in a relationship. If you find yourself avoiding making decisions, reflect on your reasons, asking, "Why am I reluctant to make a choice here? What is the fear about? What am I avoiding?" If you then choose to allow others to make the decision for you, at least it is because you have consciously decided to do so.

It is easy to make excuses or take the path of blame, whether it applies to people or circumstances. The blame-and-excuse game is comfortable, protecting you from emotional pain, from fear, or from getting out of your comfort zone. But ultimately, subconsciously, you become a victim of your fear.

You can own and live your best, most authentic life. Take personal responsibility for your decisions.

CHOOSE TO LOVE YOURSELF

The closest and most important relationship that you will ever have is with yourself. When that relationship is healthy and full of love, everything in your life takes on a new meaning. Give the relationship you have with yourself priority, nurture it, and treat it as if it were sacred—because it is! This self-love is one of the most rewarding gifts you will ever give yourself. It will transform your life and the lives of the people around you.

Have you ever asked yourself:

- Do I enjoy hanging out with myself?

- Do I love myself?

- What can I do to show myself love?

- What are my needs and how do I meet them?

- What can I do to improve my well-being?

- How can I nourish the relationship I have with myself?

Often we neglect this relationship with ourselves because most of us have not been taught how essential it is to nurture it. We have been conditioned to always think first about our relationship with others, to put their needs before ours, and to love them completely—but what about ourselves?

When you unconditionally love yourself, take care of your well-being, fulfill your needs, and put yourself first, you no longer need to seek outside approval or acceptance, and you won't look to others to satisfy your needs or to fill an emptiness within you. You know your worth and won't allow anyone to define it for you. How you appreciate, respect, and love yourself will be mirrored in how others regard you. And once you have filled your self-care and self-love "tank," as a complete being you can now share the best of yourself with others; you are not giving from an empty place but from a place of fulfillment and abundance.

How do you go about loving yourself and showing yourself love? A good place to start is by thinking about someone whom you love very much. Reflect on what you are willing to do for this person. How do you show your love? How accepting are you of this person? What mutual plans do you make? How do you speak to this person? How much do you care for their health? What do you do to make them happy? Once you're aware of how you express love and acceptance to others, start doing the same for yourself. This is especially true when you communicate with yourself—do it with as much care, kindness, and love as you can muster.

Get to know yourself, recognize your needs, forgive yourself for past decisions, learn what nourishes you, and accept and love yourself for who you are, despite what you may perceive as imperfections.

One of the things I still do if I uncover parts of myself that require extra love is to imagine my younger self. For example, when I recognize that I am seeking acceptance or validation, I imagine myself as a child, and in my mind's eye I hug her, telling her reassuringly that she is accepted and loved.

Nourish your relationship with yourself with love, respect, and compassion—because it is eternal.

CHOOSE TO OBSERVE YOURSELF

You already know how important it is to pay attention to your thoughts and emotions. Your observations will give you the opportunity to target behaviours you want to change and acquire self-knowledge and self-awareness.

The way you see yourself is reflected in the way you see others. In mirror-like fashion, you project both your flaws and good qualities onto others; your strengths are projected as their strengths, and your limitations are projected as their limitations. When you find yourself judging someone, observe yourself and ask:

- Why am judging this person?

- What is my judgment telling me about myself?

- How is this situation reflecting on me?

- What can I learn about myself in this judgment?

Become curious when you notice your urges, your needs, your excuses, and your overreactions. Observe them and get to know them by asking yourself:

- Why do I have this urge or need? Where does it come from?

- What benefits am I getting from having this urge or need?

- Why do I feel the need to make excuses for myself or my behaviours?

- Am I avoiding something? What is it? Why am I avoiding it?

- What am I getting by giving myself excuses and avoiding difficult situations?

- Why am I acting this way?

When you notice that you're taking things personally, pay attention to your behaviours and thoughts, as the situation may be something your ego wants to control. Ask yourself:

- Why am I taking this personally? Where is it coming from? How am I benefiting from it?

- What am I defending myself from?

- What identity have I created that is making me react this way?

Reflecting on your answers will help you to release or reframe subconscious ideas that are not serving you well, and to reinforce those that are.

CHOOSE YOUR OWN MEANING OF SUCCESS

Your definition of success has been conditioned and it may be causing you unnecessary suffering as you strive to live by others' standards. Be aware of your current definition of success because it can change at different stages of your life. Ask yourself:

- What does success mean to me today?

- What is my definition of success?

- How will I know when I am successful?

- What would I be doing and experiencing?

- What would I be feeling?

Live your own standards, your own beliefs and values, rather those of others or those that society has trained you to believe.

CHOOSE LOVE OVER FEAR

Fear is the most primal and powerful of human emotions and probably the one that places the greatest limitations on people. In the past, fear protected our ancestors from high-risk situations. Today, fear is more likely to be busy protecting our mental concepts and the identification we have with our ego. Because fear provides an adrenalin rush, it can often be mistaken for other, healthier emotions such as excitement and anticipation, which also heighten your senses.

Conversely, you may need to dig deep to unearth your fear(s). As you learned earlier, fear often masquerades as unpleasant emotions such as anger. For example, perhaps you are angry with your partner, who won't comply with your wish to attend a conference in a city far from you. Your partner is concerned about household expenses and thinks a distant conference is unaffordable just now. If you were asked what emotion you feel at that moment, you might say you're angry. But is that truly what you feel? If you ask yourself, "*Why* am I angry?" you might find that deep down, you are actually fearful—fearful of missing out on the conference's learning and networking opportunities, fearful of missing a chance to solidify your position in your industry, fearful of what others might think of your economic status if you're a no-show. Fear can often be found buried beneath a number of other, more readily apparent, unpleasant emotions, so examine your surface emotion carefully to find out whether it is masking some deeper, baser emotion like fear. Identifying the true emotion makes it much easier to manage.

Let's do a short exercise. Breathing deeply, take two minutes and reflect on a moment in your life when you chose fear. Where did that choice take you? How do you feel about your decision now? After you think about this moment, take two more minutes to reflect on a time when you made a choice based on love and excitement, a moment when you allowed yourself to walk into the unknown by following your heart. Now ask yourself the same questions.

What did this exercise reveal to you? Can you learn something about yourself and the consequences of your choices?

When you recognize fear in your life, with a curious mind ask yourself some of the following questions. They will help you bring more awareness to the situation.

- What am I fearful of?

- What are some reasons fear came at this point in my life?

- What is this fear protecting me from?

- What would happen if my fear were to come true?

- Could I live with the worst-case scenario?

- How would I feel if I yield to fear in my life?

- Would I regret choosing fear?

- How would I feel if I allowed fear to stop me?

- What excites me about this?

- How would I learn and grow from this situation?

- What drives my passion?

- What is my heart telling me?

- What do I feel called to do?

- What can I learn?

Fear is a strong emotion that is the underlying driver of many behaviours, so it's key to understand when it appears in your life and dissect the information it brings. Act wisely upon that information. When you recognize a feeling of simultaneous nervousness and excitement, it may at first feel like fear, but if you act on it, you could be opening the door to an excellent opportunity to learn and evolve.

Love is a powerful place from which to make choices because your heart always guides you—it knows the way.

CHOOSE TO FORGIVE

Forgiveness is an act of self-love.

Most people believe that forgiving means ignoring that the offensive conduct ever happened and forgetting the pain it caused. But actually, forgiveness is about releasing the resentment, anger, and sadness that we feel because of the behaviour of others. It is about choosing ourselves first so we can let go, heal, and move forward with peace. It is about choosing our well-being, and that is an act of self-love.

Time doesn't always erase all wounds, and you may have pain from your past that is driving your current behaviours. As an example, I can point to my relationship with my sister, who visited me in Canada some years ago. At the time we were not close. One day she hesitantly brought to my attention that she was feeling rejected by me. Her confession struck me forcefully, because I do love my sister. I reflected on my distant behaviours toward her and realized that it was caused by the pain of her bullying me as a child. I didn't realize until that moment just how much emotional pain I was harbouring, and I had unconsciously been trying to hurt her back. With this awareness, I chose to forgive her, and our relationship was transformed in incredible ways.

My experience highlights the fact that we often carry past pain that is reflected in our present behaviours, and that in forgiveness we find peace, love, and possibilities.

I urge you to forgive those who caused you pain. Visualize them in front of you as you talk with them. Also, be sure to forgive yourself for any self-destructive behaviour and decisions. As you are forgiving others and yourself, practise self-love and self-compassion.

CHOOSE YOUR HABITS

Earlier, you learned how you have been conditioned through habitual behaviours. In this section, I trust you'll come to understand that you have the choice, the opportunity, and the free will to create or change any habit. It is simple: make the decision to change and commit to it.

As you've learned, your brain is a very efficient organ. In its efficiency, it will always take the path of least resistance—which means it will favour your ingrained patterns and habits—unless you consciously set it on another path.

Your brain is not going to make it easy for you to form new habits, because your old ones, over time, have become deeply entrenched in their own neural pathways. But when you are using your power of choice, you can decide to act differently when you are facing the old habit. As soon as you notice the old desire, stop and choose your new path of action.

For instance, imagine that you want to create a new, healthy eating habit. Each time you go for groceries or to a restaurant you have the choice of which foods you will eat or buy. Notice that it is your decision and no one else's. At that moment, counteract the old habit by focusing on the reasons you want to create the new one. Stay focused on its benefits. And be sure to do it with determination, because the old patterns are strongly anchored in your brain and difficult to change. But when you do begin creating the new habit, your brain will form new neural pathways to support them, and with your persistence and determination, they will eventually become your new default.

* * *

In this third part of the book, you have learned how to get out of your mind and stop living on autopilot. You do this by mastering your emotions, by removing your four conditioned beliefs, through the power of your mind, and through your power of choice.

I encourage you to decide, with awareness, that you want to move forward to a higher level of consciousness and connect with your true essence so you can live a fulfilling life. It will not happen by staying asleep and just going through the motions of life.

You start living when you stop sleepwalking through life. As you have learned, you accomplish this by directing your thoughts, choosing your actions, guiding your responses to life's experiences, and aligning all aspects of your holistic being, nurturing them and connecting to their wisdom. You start living when you allow life to take its course and you align to its nature rather than resisting it.

In Part 4 of the book, we will delve into learning more about the wisdom of your holistic being. When you recognize and understand all of its aspects, you'll be able to nurture those areas of yourself, aligning with them so you are living fully consciously.

— KEY SUMMARY POINTS —

(1) Choose your thoughts. Only you have the power to observe your thoughts; thus, only you have the power to choose them and direct them. Choose only those that focus on love and possibilities and those that motivate you.

(2) Choose the meaning of your circumstances. You cannot control all of the events in your life; nor can you change the past. But you can select the meaning you give to those events, and you can accept them, learn from them, and forgive so that you can move forward.

(3) Choose to be grateful. Practising gratitude is a wonderful gift. It helps you keep in mind the blessings that are already surrounding you. It helps to improve your mood and well-being and supports you in moving forward during challenging circumstances.

(4) Choose a curious mindset. Approaching life with wonder helps you see different perspectives and opportunities. It also enhances your relationships, supports your career, and facilitates your personal development. You become less rigid and more flexible in your thinking.

(5) Choose your focus. Start choosing your focus rather than allowing others to direct your attention or allowing your mind to run wild. Discipline your mind by consciously directing your impulses.

(6) **Choose to be present.** Train your mind to be in the present. When you allow your mind to wander rather than being in the now, you are missing out on life. It is only in the now that you are truly alive.

(7) **Choose your response.** Every situation in your life gives you an opportunity to direct your responses. By tuning in to your emotions, you can direct them as soon you feel them rising.

(8) **Choose to take responsibility for your life.** No one else is living your life for you, so no one else will do your inner work for you; no one else will exercise or eat healthily for you. Your life is your responsibility—it is your choice to own it and live it fully.

(9) **Choose to love yourself.** The most important relationship you will ever have is with yourself. It is a sacred one! Give it priority, love and accept everything about yourself, and remember it is an act of self-love when you have the courage to change things you don't like about yourself. Fill your self-care and self-love tanks before you start giving to others, because giving from a low tank depletes you.

(10) **Choose to observe yourself.** Observing yourself supports you in uncovering your programming and your ego's behaviours. It helps you develop self-knowledge and self-awareness. Observe your reactions, your thoughts, your judgments of others. These judgments act as a mirror; what you see in others, you see in yourself.

11 **Choose your definition of success.** By choosing your own definition of success, you will be living by your own standards and not the standards others have imposed upon you.

12 **Choose love over fear.** Fear generates more fear, which traps you in a fearful cycle. Instead of yielding to it, choose love, passion, and excitement, and follow the guidance from your heart. It knows the way.

13 **Choose to forgive.** Forgiveness of others and of oneself is an act of self-love. It is not about forgetting or denying the experience. It is about releasing the associated resentment, anger, sadness, and guilt. It is about choosing your well-being over old, stale resentments.

14 **Choose your habits.** Choose to create habits that contribute to your well-being. If you have fallen into an unhealthy habit, you can override it with your conscious mind and choose a healthy one. You have the power—use it!

PRACTICE SUGGESTIONS FOR PART 3

1 **Uncover your ego's images**

Reflect on the roles you play in your life, and write them down. These can include roles in your career, in your relationships with family and with friends, in your extra curricular activities, perhaps in your volunteer work, and so on. As you identify your roles, you can also uncover your ego's "rules" and expectations for each role. Write these down too.

For instance, in my example about ego on page 84, my role was one of a healthy, athletic person. My rules were to exercise often and eat healthily. I expected myself to exercise six times a week, to always push my body in my workouts, and to maintain a diet with no carbs or sweets. I also expected the people close to me to behave similarly.

Once you've written out your roles and listed the rules and expectations you've set for each, reflect on these questions:

- Do I sometimes feel guilty if I am not complying with my own rules and expectations?

- Do I punish myself in certain ways when my behaviours do not measure up to my rules or expectations?

- Am I imposing the expectations I have for myself on others?

- Why do I expect others to behave according to my rules?

With that awareness, ask yourself:

- In which areas of my life might those rules and expectations limit me?

- In what ways might they be limiting me?

- In what ways are they supporting me?

- What impact does having those high expectations of myself and others have on me?

Remember, in my example, my ego's image was a supportive one in general, but unconsciously it was limiting me in other parts of my life.

Once you become aware of your roles, you can recognize when your ego is at play, imposing rules and expectations. At that moment, you can direct your mind, consciously decide how to move forward with your behaviours, and modify (or remove) your rules and expectations so they fully support you.

2 Practise Meditation

A regular practice of meditation will literally change your brain and literally change your life. Meditation trains your mind to attain focus and stillness. You are exercising your brain while acquiring self-knowledge and connecting to your higher self.

Meditation helps you become more in tune with yourself; it allows you to be more aware of your body, your thoughts, your inner being, to manage your emotions, to direct your behaviours, to uncover your conditioning, to heal from your past experiences, and to achieve inner peace and equanimity. Meditation will help you implement all you have learned so far.

Research has shown the vast benefits of meditation and how it alters the brain. It has also shown the great benefits it brings to one's well-being.

There are plenty of resources available to teach you different techniques of meditation. You have the choice to begin harvesting its benefits for your life. Here's a place to start:

- Sit down with both feet on the ground or cross-legged, hands on your lap.

- Set a timer. You can start with ten minutes and increase as your practice progresses.

- Take five big breaths to focus, and follow every subsequent breath in and out.

- Each time that your mind wanders, bring the focus back to your breathing, without judgment.

- Be determined to discipline your mind to continue focusing on your breath until the time is over. Harvest your power to choose your focus and direct your mind.

3 **Examine your beliefs**

When you notice that any one of the four beliefs shown in Chapter 9 is manifesting itself in your mind, you can use the questions given for your self-examination to help you have a breakthrough about that belief.

HOW TO CHANGE A HABIT IN FOUR STEPS

With determination and perseverance, you can change any habit. You simply need to make the choice and begin directing your thoughts and behaviours.

>**First step:** *Awareness.* Recognize when you are acting or about to act according to your old habit, and stop yourself immediately.
>
>**Second step:** *Ask why.* Bring into your awareness the reasons it is essential for you to stop this old habit and create a new one.
>
>**Third step:** *Conscious direction.* In your awareness, use your choice and willpower to direct the creation of a new habit.
>
>**Fourth step:** *Determination.* This is key because your brain will oppose you. Don't give up—continue working on and repeating the new habit until it becomes ingrained.

Once you become aware of your mind's resistance to creating a new habit, you can direct your thoughts to help you break through the resistance. Focus on the reasons you want to create a new habit, and use your will and determination to create it.

TWO TIPS FOR CREATING A NEW HABIT

1. Use imagery. For instance, to encourage healthy new habits, I put pictures on my fridge of nutritious and appealing foods, of other fit women, and of activities that my new lifestyle would allow me to participate in (such as hiking in the mountains). With these powerful visual reminders, it was easier to conquer my mind's resistance, work toward my heart's desire for a healthier lifestyle, and keep myself accountable.

2. Identify the benefits the old habit is giving you. Become curious and recognize how the habit is serving you. Is it providing you with comfort, gratification, escape, or something else? For example, smoking can provide a chance to socialize or a way to take a break during the day, and cigarette chemicals interact with the brain's to give quick satisfaction. Knowing where the old habit is coming from and why you depend on it will help you change it.

Changing any old pattern requires a conscious effort. You now have the steps and tips to support you in suppressing old, damaging habits and creating new, healthy ones.

— PART FOUR —

START LIVING

CHAPTER ELEVEN

WHO ARE YOU?

You exist in time, but you belong to eternity.
You are a penetration of eternity into the world of
time. You are deathless, living in a body of death.
Your consciousness knows no death, no birth.
It is only your body that is born and dies.

—Osho

Now that you understand how you can consciously direct your life (instead of allowing your subconscious mind to influence you) and stop living on autopilot, you may find yourself with a few questions:

- If I remove all my conditioning and my ego's identities, who am I?

- How am I supposed to live my life?

- From which direction I am supposed to guide my life?

We all have free will. With your free will, you can guide your life in two ways. One way is by continuing to satisfy the conditioned needs and rules of your ego, and the other is by following your heart. In your conscious awareness, you can choose to follow your heart, then allow this new awareness of your heart's desires to guide your thoughts. Use these conscious thoughts to instruct and direct your mind.

The guidance you receive from your heart is based on love; it guides you with a sense of *knowing* which decisions and actions are the right ones to take. Your heart guidance comes from your soul, your eternal self, which is your connection to the Divine.

Your mind, your heart, and your soul are all part of you, and together they play an integral part in how you experience your life. And let's not forget the body, because without your body you cannot have your human experience. Mind, body, heart, and soul—all four make up your holistic being , and when they are fully aligned, this harmonious state is known as *quantum alignment*. In the next chapters, we'll discuss the specific wisdom each of them brings to your life and how you can nourish them. But before we get to that, let's first explore an important question. Your understanding is essential as we continue along in the book.

Have you ever wondered, *Who am I?* If you haven't, this is your opportunity to explore this question. I invite you to take a few minutes to reflect, then write down your answers.

After you've done this exercise, you may find that your answers reflect a literal description of you. They may include your name, gender, age, birthplace, appearance, position at work, relationship status, beliefs and values, roles in your family and in society, achievements, academic studies, past experiences, and what you have acquired in material possessions. But are all those things and labels really who you are? Let's look at this idea in more detail.

From an early age, you learned to discover the world through your senses. You were taught to assign a meaning to everything you observed, in the process making memories and labelling your experiences so you could successfully navigate the world. You were taught how to behave, what to believe, what to think, who you should be, what you should have—you were programmed. As a result, you began to identify yourself with the outer world through these programmed perceptions and ideas. You identified with your mind, your conditioned beliefs, your experiences, your appearance, what you achieved, what you owned, your roles in life, and how people perceived you.

But if you have been conditioned in this way throughout your life, who is the real you? Are you the sum of your conditioning? Are you your physical appearance? Are you what others say you are?

It's time to recognize that all the beliefs you have about yourself are self-created descriptions in your mind of how you have known yourself to be. Many, but not all, are conditioned. They define how you go about your life and operate in the physical world. They are beliefs based on your personal history that have prompted you to live largely on autopilot. If you start observing that these conditioned beliefs are simply creations of your mind, you'll understand they are just concepts that don't really define who you are. But if that's the case, then *who are you?*

You may have already sensed who you are, recognizing your true self through the exercises you've done in this book, when you observed and directed your thoughts and felt your emotions. You can do it again right now if you choose.

I invite you to seat yourself comfortably and close your eyes. Start by taking five big breaths. Then place your hands on your heart and, very slowly, mentally scan your body, focusing on each body part from the top of your head to your toes and back. Finally, direct your attention to your heart, focus on it for ten more breaths, and sense it. Then ask, "Who am I?"

Did you become a little more aware of who you are? You are the one observing your mind and directing your thoughts. You are the consciousness guiding your focus, sensing your body, and feeling your experiences from moment to moment. You are the one who witnesses your life and recognizes your emotions. You are the awareness that feels your body's sensations, that rejoices with love and recognizes pain. You are a whole divine being. You are the observer, a soul who is watching itself living its own human experience.

Most of us were not taught how to recognize and connect with our authentic essence and live our life in this full awareness. But now you have a choice. You have the gift of free will, which allows you to decide to align with your soul and connect to your source—the Universe, your Higher Self, your Higher Power, your Energy, God, Infinite Spirit, the Creator, the Divine, or Something Greater—whatever you choose to call it.

If you observe the world around you, you'll see how wonderful the human experience is. You are living on a dreamlike planet that sustains your life. You have the capacity to experience all the shades of your emotions. You have the power to direct your thoughts and behaviours. You have the power to experience the moment and rejoice in the feeling of holding your lover or seeing a loved one happy. You can experience the feel of the rain, the touch of the wind, the smell of the air, the warmth of the sun, the majesty of nature. All of these are life's treasures, beautiful gifts that make for magnificent human experience when you partake of them through your holistic being. You have the power to appreciate all of them and, if you are consciously present, to fully experience them. You have the power to live at a higher level of consciousness and to enjoy freedom and peace.

Only you can decide whether you want to take advantage of this choice of free will. If you do, it is then up to you to do the inner work required to wake up and to live your life fully and in quantum alignment—alignment of body, mind, heart, and soul—with your source.

CHAPTER TWELVE

THE WISDOM
OF YOUR BODY

Our bodies are our gardens,
to which our wills are gardeners.
—William Shakespeare

Your body is your vehicle in this life. It is important that you nourish and love it and always proactively give it priority, not just when you find yourself unhealthy and are reminded of the importance of your health and vitality.

Let me invite you to reflect for five minutes, asking yourself:

- How well do I take care of my body?

- How do I treat it and show it respect?

- Am I nourishing it with nutritious foods?

- Am I keeping it strong through exercise?

- What more can I do to enhance its welfare?

Your body, this pillar of your holistic being, is your energy and your vitality. Your physical health is the foundation for everything that you do in life. It influences all your undertakings. Without good health, you will not be able to fully experience and enjoy the outside world. You need to give your body what it requires so it supports you and helps you enjoy your life.

What does healthy living mean for you? It's important to choose your own path to good health and not let society define it for you. As part of leading a conscious life, you want to recognize how good health will improve your life; it's then your responsibility to take action and make health decisions accordingly. I encourage you to follow these guidelines and, if you already haven't, start giving your body what it needs.

- **Get enough sleep.** The expectations you put on yourself and the demands of society may often cause you to cut back on sleep, thinking you need to maximize the use of your waking hours. But in reality, you do this at the expense of your health, performance, productivity, and peace of mind. Most adults need a minimum of seven to nine hours of sleep a night to function at their highest level.

- **Get your body moving.** Being active strengthens your cardiovascular and immune systems, increases your energy, and improves your mood. Exercise also reduces your stress and supports your brain function and cognitive health.

- **Drink lots of water.** Healthy fluids help flush toxins out of your body and maintain its equilibrium.

- **Eat your vegetables and fruits.** Healthy foods provide your body with the nutrients to function efficiently. When choosing food, let nature be your guide. Select whole foods and raw foods whenever you can, and keep chemically processed, packaged foods to a minimum or don't eat them at all.

- **Meditate.** Meditation will help you reduce stress and anxiety, which directly benefits your physical and mental health.

FOOD AND DRINK

Your eating habits have been conditioned and your choices of food reflect that conditioning. Become more aware of your eating habits, and be in tune with your body's needs. Pay attention to what your body is telling you, and modify your diet accordingly. Feelings of sluggishness, fatigue, or lack of motivation could be caused by a poor diet, a food allergy, or a lack of sleep.

Do your homework and learn more about the food you eat and why you eat it. Take responsibility for your food decisions each time you go to the fridge, buy groceries, or dine in a restaurant. Choose consciously and not out of habit.

YOUR BODY AND EMOTIONS

Follow the wisdom of your body by noticing your cravings and your impulses to eat. They will provide you with insight into subconscious emotions that might be hiding deep-rooted psychological triggers. For instance, a common habit is relying on comfort food to fill some kind of lack in one's life.

YOUR BODY AND MOOD

How you hold yourself can influence your emotional state; in the same way, your emotional state can influence how you hold your body. Knowing this, you can use your body to contribute to your emotional well-being. Something as simple as putting on a smile can brighten up your day.

Your body posture can reflect what is going within you emotionally. An upright bearing shows strength and confidence; a slumped-over position can indicate distress, insecurity, or self-doubt. But while you can definitely use your body to improve your mood, be aware that this is one way of covering up an unresolved trigger that needs to be addressed; otherwise it will manifest itself again.

YOUR BODY AND STILLNESS

You can use your body to help you bring stillness to your mind—for instance, through the regular practice of meditation.

Even if you find that meditation isn't for you, you can use your body when you need to find calmness at any given moment by simply breathing deeply and focusing solely on the physical sensations of your breath as you inhale and exhale.

CHAPTER THIRTEEN

THE WISDOM

OF YOUR MIND

When you are observing the old self, you are no longer the program, now you are the consciousness observing the program and that's when you begin to objectify your subjective self.

—Dr. Joe Dispenza

A ccessing your mind's wisdom is possible only when it is still and calm and open, and when you are consciously directing it away from its past conditioning. When you quiet the noise of your thoughts and emotions, you have the ability to direct your mind, with guidance from your heart, and become the active creator of your life. Connecting with the wisdom of your mind is one of the first steps toward self-realization.

Accessing your conscious mind can also help you become aware of information buried in your subconscious that may be driving your ego and your conditioned behaviours. This information can include harmful beliefs and self-destructive behaviours, ongoing negative experiences, and traumatic events. Uncovering this information will help you heal and move forward from those experiences with love and compassion, for yourself and others.

To cultivate the wisdom of your mind, start by monitoring your ego so when it manifests itself, you do not react to its impulses—you guide it instead. You do this by detaching yourself from your self-identification with your ego, your beliefs, your thoughts, the roles you play in life, and your ideas of who you are. For instance:

- When you observe a non-productive thought or recognize a limiting belief, you can detach from any of them by simply telling yourself, "Interesting thought/belief I just had. Wonder where it's coming from?"

- When you notice one of your ego's controlling reactions, you can detach from it by telling yourself, "There's my ego at play again. I'm curious. What's going on with my ego now?"

You can detach from any of these when you consciously become an objective observer of your life.

Next, examine your unpleasant emotions, no matter how hard this may be. These emotions can help you uncover the triggers that are prompting you to react fearfully or in other harmful ways. Once you've uncovered these triggers and are fully aware of them, you're on your way to freeing yourself of them and leading a more peaceful life.

Remember, your mind can keep you living fearfully or it can keep you living fearlessly. It can keep you suffering or it can keep you in harmony. You have the ability to choose which you nurture.

Your mind likes to plan, to strategize, to comprehend because it innately craves certainty. Paradoxically, because your mind doesn't like uncertainty, it will seek to control and keep you limited within the boundaries of your status quo, knowledge, and comfort zone, even if this is detrimental to your well-being. Each time you are placed out of your familiar zone, your mind will become uncertain and very uncomfortable; it will do everything it can to return you to the safety of your conditioning and your ego's images of yourself. But with willpower and intentional thought, you can get your mind on board and leverage its wisdom to support you in your life's journey.

For example, years ago when I launched my company, I felt uneasy and hesitant because of all the uncertainties that come with launching a new business. As I noticed anxiety rising within me, I chose to deliberately guide my mind. I directed my self-conversation to focus on the parts of me that value growth and learning. I focused on giving my mind the certainty it needed by concentrating on the positive actions I was taking for my business. I guided my mind to stillness, which allowed me to be creative and enjoy the process of building something I am passionate about.

Be conscious and aware of the information you feed your mind, because it shapes the way you think and reprograms your subconscious. Feed your mind with information that adds value to your life, expands your knowledge, and helps you grow.

YOUR MIND AND YOUR BODY

The relationship between the mind and the body is reciprocal. Through your mind, you can make your body stronger and healthier, and when your body is fit and healthy, you'll feel better mentally and emotionally.

Studies using a placebo have demonstrated that your mind alone has healing power. Many cases have been documented of people healing themselves simply by the power of their mind. But it is a two-way street; if you can heal yourself with constructive thoughts, you can also create physical and emotional suffering for yourself with unconstructive thoughts. With or without your awareness, your thoughts are influencing your well-being, so why not consciously guide them?

By using your mind, you can train your body to go beyond what it has perceived its limits to be. When your body complains that it has reached its limits, giving direction to your mind can override those complaints, allowing you to keep training and becoming stronger. As your body gets stronger so does your mind. It's a cycle of positive reinforcement.

CHAPTER FOURTEEN

THE WISDOM OF
YOUR HEART

*Your vision will become clear only when you can look
into your own heart. Who looks outside, dreams;
who looks inside, awakes.*

—Carl Jung

Your heart is your guide, the compass that points the way into a new world of passion, excitement, joy, and flow. It leads you through your life with kindness, compassion, and connection. It directs your life in the highest way, based on love.

Your heart guides you with love, and your conditioned mind guides you with fear. Your heart knows what is best for your evolution, but when it leads you into the unknown your mind jumps in to seek control. Your conditioned mind and your ego are closely connected. Your conditioned mind's tendency is to prevent your heart from leading; it wants you to live according to your ego's wishes and ignore your heart's desires. Your ego induces you to think only about yourself instead of serving others and contributing to the greater good of all.

How do you recognize when your heart is guiding? It is a sense of *knowing*, at your core, that there are no questions or doubts about your decision. But even if you *know* with certainty which path to take, your conditioned mind may still harbour fear and reservations, pointing out all the risks and creating excuses to avoid your heart's guidance. Sometimes you feel torn by the situation— one part of you desires it, and the other has doubts. Your heart and mind can throw you into a dilemma, with excitement tugging one way and hesitation another. Ultimately, you have free will to decide which one you want to follow, using the suggestions in this book to help you more objectively evaluate these mixed messages.

The wisdom of your heart is telling you to keep your heart open. When you do this, love will freely flow through you without the restrictions imposed by fear, and you'll feel a wondrous sense of peace and ease within you and all around you. Keep an open heart and have the *courage* to follow it.

You may already sense when your heart is open, but how can you be sure? Think of something you love to do. Close your eyes and sense how your heart feels while thinking of your passion. What you are feeling is an open heart; stay with that awareness for a few minutes. Next, think about something you are fearful of, close your eyes, and sense how it feels. What you are feeling is a closed heart. Reflect on the difference between both experiences. Now you can recognize what your heart is telling you.

Your heart tends to close not only when you are fearful, but also when someone or something triggers you or you face a psychological threat. For instance, think about a time when one of your loved ones said something hurtful to you and you became upset. In that moment, your heart closed and your ego put you in a defensive mode, preventing you from acting with compassion or kindness.

As you have learned, when something triggers you, you first feel the emotion, and this is when you will feel your heart closing.

In that moment of awareness, carefully choose your response and keep your heart open while you examine your emotional reactions and your triggers. Repeat to yourself, "Breathe, breathe deeply, relax, and keep your heart open." Connecting with the wisdom of your heart will help you more easily navigate the situation because you will be, in your awareness, directing your mind and not allowing fear to overwhelm you.

When you feel the call from your heart but notice your conditioned mind is giving you excuses and prompting doubts, in that moment, listen to your inner voice and understand what it is telling you. Be curious about it and understand the needs of your mind. Is it your ego that wants you to conform to a certain image? Is it your conditioning or habits that want you to stay in your comfort zone? Pay attention to your emotions because they reveal what is going on in your mind. If it is fear, detach from it and objectively examine how true it is to you. Ask yourself:

- Is this fear mine or is it coming from someone else?

- Is it coming from my ego or my conditioning?

- What are my options?

- Why is it showing up in my life now?

Face the fear and, with courage, allow yourself to imagine the worst-case scenario. Ask yourself:

- Would I be able to live with this or with the knowledge that I didn't go after my heart's desires?

With this reflection, you can make decisions. When you choose to follow your heart, remember that your conditioned mind is using fear only to try to protect you, and with compassion you can guide it through the process. Keep in mind that fear is an intrinsic part of being human. All creatures were designed with fear as an inherent part of their makeup as a means of self-protection. It's when you allow your conditioned mind and/or other people to instill fear that you need to consciously work on redirecting it, and follow your heart instead.

Connecting with your heart takes practice. Start small as you begin to learn what it is telling you. For instance, let's say you feel in your heart a desire to go out for dinner, take time for yourself, take a trip, or do something else that you know will contribute to your well-being. You want to do this thing, but you feel hesitant or guilty—your conditioned mind is holding you back from what will bring you joy and make you happy. This is the time to observe your thoughts, notice the resistance, and figure out the reasons for it. Perhaps you fear being seen sitting alone in a restaurant, or perhaps you feel you can't afford the time and money for a trip. Use as much objectivity as you can to explore whether these reasons are truly valid or whether they are just conditioned excuses.

Accustom yourself, in your conscious awareness, to listen to and follow your heart's guidance. Choose to go after things that take you out of your comfort zone and into the unknown. In this way, you will gradually become comfortable with being uncomfortable. To further connect with your heart, act with kindness, compassion, and gratitude to yourself, to others, and to nature. Be of service to the world. Prioritize your choices in terms of what your heart wants, and you'll find yourself doing more of the things you are passionate about and that bring you joy.

KNOW YOUR INTENTION

You can approach something with two different intentions. These intentions can come from either the heart or the conditioned mind, the former based on love and the latter on fear and protection of your status quo. Both options carry a different level of energy and have different driving factors.

For example, you can exercise with different intentions. One comes from the heart, from loving your body and feeling healthy, and the other comes from fear, from disliking your body and feeling uncomfortable in it. The approach that stems from the heart will support and motivate you while the one that stems from fear will hinder you and hold you back.

Observe whether some of your thoughts, beliefs, or activities are coming from a place of fear. As you now know, this generally expresses itself as emotional pain, shame, embarrassment, or anger. This awareness will help you understand the origins of your behaviours, and then give them a new meaning. You can create new beliefs that support you.

CHAPTER FIFTEEN

THE WISDOM

OF YOUR SOUL

True mastery can be gained by letting things go their
own way. It cannot be gained by interfering.

—Lao Tzu

Your soul is what connects you with the Divine. It is the part of you that is eternal and universal. When you are self-aware, in tune with your inner self, and in alignment with your Divine source, you can more easily recognize how your soul guides your heart. Once you are aware of this, you can direct your conscious mind to follow your heart.

The wisdom of your soul will help you discover the unknown, guiding you as you strive to realize your full potential. By following the purpose of your soul, you will reach higher levels of consciousness and love. Courage, trust, and faith are required to follow your soul's guidance as it flows through your heart. But once you decide to follow it, you'll be able to navigate your life without seeking to control exactly how it will unfold. You will step into your *inner knowing*, willingly relinquishing control, surrendering to the flow of life, and allowing it to evolve in its own perfect way.

At first, as you follow your soul's guidance through listening to your heart, your conditioned mind will want to take back control because the new, unknown path is uncomfortable to your ego. This is a process of surrendering, letting go, and trusting in your Higher Source. When you do this, you can allow your life's circumstances to evolve as they are meant to and navigate them without resistance, knowing you are fully supported, guided, loved, and protected by your Higher Self. In the face of any of life's uncertainties, it's important to maintain your faith and trust and be fearless in the face of the unknown.

When you follow your soul, you are opening yourself to a world of opportunities and ways of expression where there are no boundaries. You start living a life in the flow of love, a life in which there is no suffering, a life that stretches beyond your imagination. You get to know what it really means to live with purpose and experience inner peace.

Your soul will take you where you are meant to be. The path unfolds as you travel it, and you see different perspectives as you learn and evolve. Along the way, you become open to more opportunities for growth and self-realization, so the process reinforces itself.

THE SCHOOL OF LIFE

What a beautiful gift it is to view life from the perspective that we are here to learn and grow, that we are enrolled in the school of life. When you see life from this perspective, each experience becomes an opportunity to learn. You approach life with flexibility, surrender, and acceptance. This perspective helps you honour your own life as well as accept other people's choices because they too are in this life to learn. You will begin to understand that every-thing is where it is supposed to be, that everything is unfolding in perfect ways for your growth and evolution.

I am not suggesting that your life will be magical every mo-ment of every day. Certain events may cause you to feel so broken inside that you cannot see the light. This is to be expected, and it's a great opportunity for you to connect with your Source, embrace it, and let yourself be guided with an open heart and an open mind. With this perspective you can ask yourself, "What can I learn from this?" and seek to understand what your experience is teaching you. Ask your Higher Self to guide and support you through the experience. There is always a gift to be found in all circumstances. See yourself as a student, brimming with curiosity.

ALIGN WITH THE FLOW OF LIFE

Most people think they are in control of their life, but life just hap-pens, and every single decision that you make as it unfolds shapes how you experience it. You navigate your life, making choices as you are faced with your experiences, and you have free will to surrender or resist. You can choose to follow the higher wisdom of your soul or keep blindly seeking to control how your life unfolds.

Life is always in flow, continually changing and evolving. You can learn from it or fight it. Imagine for a moment that life is like an ever-changing, flowing river. As it encounters obstacles, it changes it course and does not resist or fight them. It flows around obstacles in its path with patience and ease, unconstrained by its surroundings. It adapts.

Approach your life as if it were flowing water, and learn to adapt to its vicissitudes instead of resisting or fighting them.

CONNECT TO YOUR SPIRITUALITY

I invite you to recall a time when you were observing the night sky, or seeing a majestic landscape or a peaceful beach, or holding a newborn child. In those moments, did you experience a feeling of awe and wonder? Did you feel that there might be so much more than just what your senses can perceive? Did you feel that perhaps there is something much bigger out there—a higher power or a vibrational energy field that encompasses everything, including us? If you did, at that moment you were experiencing your spirituality, your loving connection with everything in the Universe.

Spirituality is not about religion. Rather, it is about connecting and aligning with the truth of who you are.

Spirituality is about connecting to everything and everyone. It is about realizing that we are all part of something greater, something beyond the material world and the physical experience. It is about understanding that we are all *one* in this experience, that we are part of the same Divine Source. It is about connecting with our Creator.

As I grew up, I always had faith that there was something greater, something that created us all. I was raised Catholic, and I duly prayed to the man with the white beard, looking to connect with Him and believing that He was someone outside of me. I now know that our Creator is not in the clouds watching over us, waiting to punish us. We are of God, God is present in our hearts and in our souls, in every single person and every living creature. We are all of part of the Infinite Spirit. It is everything and everywhere.

But many of us have lost track of our spirituality, of our purpose here on earth. We have disconnected from our souls and from our innate divinity. The Divine is within us, though, waiting to be recognized. It is up to us to willingly connect and align with the Infinite Spirit and realign with who we truly are.

When you connect with your spirituality and seek to listen to your soul, you raise your consciousness and bring awareness to who you truly are. You awaken from your sleeping state to the realization that you were living on autopilot, and you start truly living your life experience.

Everyone connects with their spirituality in different ways. For me, it began by discovering my conditioning through my emotional reactions and recognizing when my ego was manifesting itself. I started making conscious decisions, staying present, and meditating. I stood with my faith when things didn't go the way I expected. Often, I resisted the flow of life and suffered because of it, but as I gradually learned from my experiences, my resistance grew weaker and weaker.

I encourage you to find the best way to connect with your own spirituality. Perhaps yours will take the form of a meditation practice, or a religious practice, or being in nature, or plant-medicine ceremonies, or reading books on spirituality, or studying neuroscience and quantum physics, or simply the realization that you are not your ego. Choose the form of spirituality that speaks to you and guides you in connecting to your soul, to your Creator, to the Infinite Spirit—always with complete respect for others' choices.

Remember, we humans do not live in a vacuum. Every person, every creature, and all of nature is part of the Divine. We are not separate from one another; each decision we make affects everything and everyone surrounding us.

We are living our lives on a beautiful planet where everything is interconnected and everything is essential to sustain each of our lives. We share our planet with every other living and natural thing—humans, animals, plants, land, water—and all of these deserve respect, love, and care. Living in harmony with these other entities goes far beyond our own human benefit.

We, as humans, have the unique gift of free will. It gives us the ability to raise our consciousness, and to align with our soul and with the Infinite Spirit. We have the distinctive ability to consciously take care of one another and the world around us. I invite you to live your life in the flow of love and to spread that love all around you. We are all *one*, from one Divine Source.

—— PART 4: KEY SUMMARY POINTS ——

Quantum align all the parts of you

You are the observer of your life; you are the awareness that is experiencing itself in this physical world. Quantum aligning means uniting all the parts of yourself—body, mind, heart, and soul. From this oneness, start experiencing your life in its flow, without limitations, and expressing yourself in your full consciousness. When you nourish all these parts of you, you will evolve, making quantum leaps in your thinking and going beyond your conditioning into a conscious way of living, where you will find greater well-being, love, happiness, and purpose.

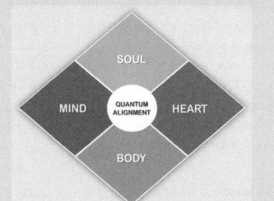

① The wisdom of your body

Your body is your physical manifestation, the vehicle through which you are experiencing life. It is essential that you nourish it, exercise it, respect it, and provide it with all that it needs to maintain its health and vitality.

2 The wisdom of your mind

Your mind's wisdom becomes apparent only when you are consciously directing it. The creation and the quality of your life is a reflection of your thought patterns. The emotions you experience are also a mirror of your thoughts. Without managing your thoughts and emotions, you will only react to life's circumstances instead of proactively navigating them. You have the power to direct your mind to achieve a state of emotional stillness and equanimity, and thus experience greater enjoyment in your life.

3 The wisdom of your heart

The wisdom of your heart comes from your soul speaking through it, guiding you to fulfill your life's purpose, and with this guidance you can lead your mind. Your heart shows you the path to experiencing life in a new state of calm, happiness, and love. The wisdom of your heart tells you to keep it open during difficult circumstances or when someone triggers you. Your heart also invites you to prioritize the things that make you happy and that bring light to your life.

4 The wisdom of your soul

Your soul is the eternal part of you, the part of the Infinite Spirit that is in you, in all of us and in everything.

In connecting with your soul, you are surrendering to the flow of life and allowing it to take its course without resistance. As you go about your life in alignment with your soul, you see everything as an opportunity to learn and continue with your evolution. Your soul will take you to discover the unknown, the possible, and things your mind hasn't yet conceived of.

* * *

With your free will, you have the power to choose to harness the wisdom of all parts of you and to follow your soul's journey, connecting and in alignment with your Source and contributing to the well-being of all.

YOUR NEXT STEPS

If this book has inspired you to live a more conscious, mindful, purposeful, and authentic life, and if you are interested in further exploring and fast-tracking your growth and evolution, you can choose not to do it alone. I can support you through one-on-one conscious leadership coaching and group workshops.

LEADERSHIP COACHING

What exactly is this type of coaching? Becoming a conscious leader is about changing the conditioned paradigm of how we see leadership. As a society, we have been taught to see a leader as someone who is in charge of guiding a group of people, whether it is in a country, a company, or a community group.

Conscious leadership is not only about viewing yourself as a leader, but about leading your own life first, consciously and from within. It is about doing the inner work required, which will allow you to lead authentically and powerfully in all your undertakings while consciously living your best life. It is about connecting with your highest potential and living fearlessly. When you become a conscious leader, you see yourself wholly and holistically. You are self-aware, you know who you are at your core, and you are emotionally intelligent. You are not bounced around by life circumstances or other people's behaviours. You are objective because you are aware of your biases, and you don't allow your survival reactions to take over your behaviours. You consciously direct your actions and manage situations with a calm mind that is open to others' perspectives. You live your life with purpose, happiness, and peace, while contributing to the well-being of the world. When you live your own life in these conscious, healthy ways, you can be a highly effective type of leader. You cannot lead others efficiently if you are not leading yourself first.

In our coaching sessions, we focus on developing your conscious connection with your inner self, exploring your strengths and areas of improvement, becoming aware of your potential, and closing the gaps between where you are and where you want to be in your leadership roles. You can also visit my personal website for upcoming group workshops and other resources, and sign up for my newsletter.

CORPORATE SOLUTIONS

Through my company, Quantum Thinking, I work with leaders to develop a conscious way of thinking that effectively and sustainably responds to change and challenges in the business environment. I teach the concepts in this book in a practical manner to people in the corporate world, where I tailor them to apply specifically to a business environment.

The workshop I've designed has practical exercises and workplace examples that show how leaders and others in the corporate environment can remove subconscious limitations they may be placing on themselves, change old, conditioned ways of thinking to more conscious, thoughtful ones, and get out of their own way to foster a more productive, trusting, positive work environment.

If you are interested in this workshop, in having me present a talk to your group, or in conscious leadership executive coaching, please contact me through my corporate website at www.quantum-thinking.ca or my personal site at www.claudiavelandia.com.

ACKNOWLEDGEMENTS

With so much love in this moment, I am most grateful to my younger self for making the decision to look within and work on herself. It has been a beautiful journey, and continues to be.

Thank you to my teachers and coaches. I also wish to thank each person and each circumstance I've encountered in my life for their teachings and for helping me evolve.

To Claude, for the endless hours he spent with me working on reviewing the manuscript of this book, for his critical mind, for the insightful reflections, and for the laughs.

To Mark, for his support on my journey and believing in me when I didn't believe in myself.

To my best friend and lovely sister, Carolina, for all your support, cheerleading, inspiration, and courage. Love you, sister!

To Alex, for providing me with the space to heal and grow.

To Darren, Kenda, and Monica, for their feedback and helpful suggestions in the early stages of this book.

To all my friends around the world who have supported and loved me throughout my life and this journey.

To my family, for their support and love.

To my editor, Arlene Prunkl, for her love and dedication to my ideas and my book.

And of course, to my parents for giving me a kick-start in this amazing life, for their love and support, and for allowing me to *be* myself and *do* my life my way. Love you both, very much!

ABOUT THE AUTHOR

Claudia Velandia, MBA, MA, BEng, is also a certified professional coach. Through conscious leadership coaching, she has helped many people by empowering them to discover their highest potential and to harness the power that comes from conscious thinking, self-awareness, and self-knowledge. She is the founder of Quantum Thinking, which helps leaders and teams develop new ways of thinking so they can effectively and sustainably respond to change and challenges in the business environment. Leaders learn how to achieve greater productivity, engagement, fulfillment, and profitability for all stakeholders and for the world.

Claudia was born in Colombia, pursued her education and career in Europe, and later settled in Canada. Her international background and personal experiences have equipped her with a global perspective and an understanding of the human psyche that are both essential to her work. Prior to founding Quantum Thinking, she had developed a successful international career, working for renowned global technology companies in demanding, highly competitive environments.

Claudia's greatest passion is to bring personal leadership and growth to every aspect of her life. She firmly believes that developing consciousness in one's life along with working on one's inner self will bring inner peace, joy, love, success, and fulfillment. She loves to spend time outdoors and enjoys reading, exercising, meditating, and learning.

Why does Claudia do what she does? *Because she is inspired to inspire people to connect and align with their souls so they can experience life fully, without limitations, and together contribute to the well-being of the world.*

Find out more about Claudia and follow her on:

Instagram: www.instagram.com/claudialivingnow
LinkedIn: www.linkedin.com/in/claudiavelandia
Website: www.claudiavelandia.com

Find out more about Quantum Thinking:

Website: www.quantum-thinking.ca

Thank you for reading my book. A final request, please ...

If you've learned something from this book that has helped you raise your awareness, step out of your conditioned mind, and stop living on autopilot, if you are inspired to live your life fully and without limitations, please help me to extend this message to others so that together we can contribute to the well-being of each person in the world.

It is my plea to you to discuss what you've learned from this book with your friends, family, and colleagues. **Furthermore, you can support me, as a self-published author, in getting the word out by leaving an honest and helpful review on Amazon, letting other readers know what you thought of the book.**

I have a vision for the world. I genuinely believe that each of us can live with purpose and happiness. It is in each person's power to create a peaceful world that is driven by love, a world where we all care about one another and each of us contributes to the well-being of the whole. To live in this way we need only to look within, work on ourselves, align with our true natures, and live consciously.

Thank you for your support!